How To Create Your Own Murder Mystery Party

By: Joseph J. Franco

For everyone who said
"Hey, this was fun,
you should write a book"

Table Of Contents

Introduction

When my wife and I decided we were going to throw a big Halloween party for the first time, I thought it would be fun to include a murder mystery type of game. I first looked into the 'boxed' type of murder mystery games. In these games, which you can buy at the store, everyone plays a different character detailed on cards and follows a predetermined script. Sometimes, the murderer does not even know they are the murderer until the end. I really did not like that approach, it lacked creativity and originality. I decided that writing my own custom designed murder mystery, during which everyone got to be himself or herself, would be much more fun. By designing a murder mystery around the people coming to the party, everyone could get more involved, get to know each other and not face the shyness issue of acting out a part.

It has been a number of parties since then and every year the murder mystery has been a blast. People look forward to our Halloween parties every year and talk about them for a while after. You will be surprised how caught up in the game people will get, how sneaky some of your friends can be and how quickly some of them will stab each other in the back; all in the name of fun, of course. You get to sit back and watch your whole story unfold as people solve your puzzles, find your clues and accuse each other of murder-nothing can be predicted!

The basis of this book is to help you write your own murder mystery games, help you explore and exercise your creative side, give you a number of ways to stimulate ideas and give you party ideas you can use, build on to, combine, etc. The party ideas range in creation complexity and play difficulty. We will cover both types in later chapters. You, of course, can determine the difficulty level of the game.

When you create your own game, the only limits are your imagination (and maybe your budget if you really get into it). The game can be set up for any amount of people, since you are the one designing it. Your mystery can deal with any topic, from a murder surrounding the Wall Street stock market scene to a murder set up in a fantasy world with witches and goblins. There are no rules on subject matter, anything can be incorporated into a game. The game can be played free style, which means everyone is themselves, people can be predetermined characters, become characters as the game progresses or you can combine any and all of the games styles during one game. It would be fun to test out your players' acting skills and have their characters change as the night goes on. You can set it up that your guests even come in predetermined costumes if you liked that aspect of 'canned' games. If you want a predetermined script, that is up to you as well. Personally I like the game to develop on its own as the night goes on, the game becomes very dynamic without any set script. You really have no idea how it will play out or what people are going to do.

I have always done the murder mystery game during Halloween, but there are no rules saying you can not just decide in July to host a murder mystery. Have a big dinner, some music and some fun, and of course, a murder. You can even go as far as not telling them it is going to be a murder mystery party, let them find the 'body' or a clue when your guests arrive. These games have always been fun, challenging and a great way for people to meet and socialize. These types of games can also be great for children's parties, make it a little more light hearted, or even take out the whole idea of a murder in the first place. The game could center around a robbery or a missing person. If you enjoy throwing parties, like games and have a little bit of a creative side, then you are on the right track.

If you want to skip ahead and take a look at "Sample Game One", go ahead, it will give you an idea of a very simple game and give you the basic idea of the structure. This game is the same structure as the "Quick game". If you choose to read over "Sample Game One" now, don't worry if you don't understand everything, it will make sense after you read the relevant chapters. If you are going to use the Quick game option, just follow the directions and you will be on your way.

Getting Started

Lets begin with how a game typically can proceed. The basic game play can vary depending on your personal preferences, the type of murder mystery you created, number of guest, etc. This chapter will explain how I have set up some games in the past. Remember this is just a basic framework on game play, not the plot or the puzzles.

The first detail that is needed to start, and one of the most fun parts of the games, is that the murderer is one of the guests. They <u>know</u> they are the killer and will be trying to protect themselves. I typically do not tell the murderer who they are until the time of the party; this will avoid any slips of the tongue previous to the party. This approach also means that you must have a back up murderer in case something goes wrong and that person does not show-up at the party, but more about that later.

Once all your guest have arrived, set yourself up in an area that is private, where the other guests can't hear you talking. Ask one of your guests to randomly call another guest to be the first to talk to you. At this point you explain the basic rules of the game, explaining to them that the murderer is another one of the guests and they know they are the murderer. Clarify anything about how the game works, do's and don'ts, any safety issues, places that are off-limits during the game, how to win if you play with a win option, etc. I typically have a rule sheet that I write up and pass out. Examples of these are included in each of the sample games. Also give the players any starting clues or story lines they will need to get them going.

Once you are done with that person, send them out, and tell them to call in another person until all your guests have been briefed. Another detail to keep in mind, is that you need to spend about the same time with everyone. Explaining the role to the murderer might take more time and your players might get suspicious if they notice someone is spending a lot of time with you. After your second year doing this, and maybe even the first year, people will take notice if you spend ten minutes talking to so-and-so, but you only spent two minutes talking to everyone else. So to cover yourself, stagger times on purpose or run long when talking to people who are not the murderer. If you begin doing murder mysteries on a regular basis, people will begin to look for any indication of who the murderer could be.

While talking to the Murderer I explain to them what they have done (story plot) and why. I tell them their job is to lie, mislead people, find and hide clues (more about that later) and do basically whatever they need to do-other than destroying clues, cheat in a way to spoil the game, etc-to keep people from knowing who they are. This is really a fun part to watch, as you will see sides of people that you never knew existed. You might be surprised with the very creative ways people devise to throw people off their tracks.

A good example of this was during one of the games that took place outside. It was evening, and all the outdoor lighting was off. I had given out four flashlights. Everyone had to team up, to use a flashlight, as there were about twenty people. The person playing the murderer was able to repeat-ably steal away the flashlights undetected. This was a party during which the murderer would drop off the clues he or she found at a predetermined place, as not to totally stop the game. Each time I would go to the 'pick up zone', there were clues and flashlights. I would overhear people saying "Hey, who has the other flashlights?", "Hey, where are all the flashlights". As you can imagine, this made searching a dark yard very difficult.

During your briefing also state that if anyone thinks they know who the murderer is, try to keep it to themselves. Secrecy keeps the game fun for everyone else. You can also give out prizes. If the murderer goes undetected he/she wins, if someone figures out who the murderer is, they win. This prize system is personal preference once again. I usually will give out first and second prizes and an acting award if applicable.

Once everyone has been briefed, the game begins. This way everyone starts at the same time and no one has any advantage. At this point, people will begin searching for clues, solving puzzles and whatever needs to be done. People typically will start forming groups, and as the game goes on, traitors will start crossing over.

Your role in the game is basically to observe, pace the game, dispense clues, answer questions, etc. You also need to pay attention to how the game is moving along. Let's say your game is based on your guests finding clues. These clues will then be put together to solve the mystery, reveal the killer and any other related information. If your players find too many clues too fast, the game will end too quickly. If they are having trouble finding/solving clues your guests might get frustrated and bored. Various ways to 'time' the game are covered in detail later.

As the night is coming to a close, have everyone write down who they think the murderer is, why they did it, and any other details they know about the murder, plot, etc. I have everyone sit around and I read

4

these off one by one. This is a lot of fun, as some of the things people will come up with are really funny. There have been times when I wondered if certain people were even playing the same game as everyone else. Once the answers have all been read, I ask the murderer to stand up. It's always fun when it is someone's spouse or boyfriend/girlfriend, and the murderer did a good enough job to keep it even from them. If everything goes well for the guests, and bad for the murderer, more than one person will have figured out whom the murderer is. This is a tie and is the reason I ask everyone to give me details about the murder and story. The person who provides the most detail about the plot wins.

Game Set Up

We will go through the initial game set up in a brief step by step procedure. Each item discussed will then be broken out in detail in following chapters specific to that item.

First you will need to come up with a story line/motive. I have listed these together because I found it easier in the long run to think of these both at the same time. You can always come up with a story, such as a romance or a treasure hunt theme and then throw a murder in, but in the beginning it might be easier to think of them as one. The initial story line should just be a basic idea, since a number of details will come to you during design. Keep in mind you are creating a murder mystery, so you want the basic plot to be flexible as to give you room to add in clues and puzzles.

A few simple examples of typical murder mystery story line are:
- Murder for inheritance.
- Murder for jealousy.
- Murder for sacrifice.

If you look at that small list and think for a little while, I am sure ideas will start coming to you. The first example game does not fall under any of these. The murderer simply wanted to protect their career.

Once you have your story/motive, it is time to decide how the killer will murder his victim and what they did with the body. In my first example, I had a stuffed dummy that I made. You can use a paper cut out and go really cheap and simple, or you could just have a ghost and don't worry about a body. Ghosts could leave spooky messages around the house telling of their fate. Once again, there are no limits to how your imagination can expand on this. Maybe the victim's soul was put inside your dog or cat, now they can be a part of the party too!

Your next issue is that of the murder weapon. In the first example I used a fireplace poker. Take a look around your house, most anything could be used as a weapon. Pretty scary when you think about it.

Whichever way you decide to go, remember you will need a body or explanation and possibly a murder weapon. If someone is drowned or choked with bare hands, there might not be actual weapons to be found.

At this point you have a story line, motive, cause of death, possible body and a possible weapon. Now its time to start thinking about how your guests are going to go about solving the mystery. Once again, I cannot stress how open this is to creativity. This is where the fun begins for everyone. You can have physical clues, riddles, math puzzles, word puzzles, etc. This is also one of the places where you can determine how hard the game is, and how many clues you need to have depending on the size of your party. The only criteria I suggest is that these are related to your story. There is nothing that can put more of a damper on things than when a player solves a puzzle or finds a clue, and it makes no sense whatsoever relative to the game.

Sometimes the best way to fill in the details is to reverse engineer the solving of the game. I usually start out with the question "How do I want them to discover who the murderer is?" In the majority of the parties I have done so far, this was accomplished by finding clues that would reveal letters of the murderers name, either first or last depending on how common either name was. If the intended murderer has the only first name in the game that contains the letter 'z', use their last name. Another approach is to make the clue that reveals the letter 'z' very hard or a number of clues must be solved to lead to it. In the first example you will see (page 22), the murderer was identified by elimination and/or physical evidence (a pin they were wearing). Also, it is always better to have too many clues than too few. As I will cover in more detail later, you can time a game not only by how hard the clues are, but how many there are. You can simply hold some clues back to slow a game or put more clues out to speed it up.

Once you have decided on the approximate number of clues you want, you can begin brainstorming new ideas on how to actually reveal these clues to your players. This also opens many doors. Most of the paper type clues are hidden around the house and/or property. There might be clues hanging from tree branches, hidden under just about anything movable, etc. Other times they are out in plain sight, the players might not even realize that a painting on the wall is, or contains a clue. Maybe the players need to find another clue mentioning a painting. In the sample games I have included, you will see many different ways I have made clues available to the players.

Your story will start to come together and depending on how complex your mystery is, you will see the loose ends start to develop. You must close any loose ends in your story. You will need to review the completed murder mystery at least three times to make sure you have all your times correct, that your puzzles lead to the right clues, etc. Also make sure you have included all the clues that are needed. Check for any contradictions or things you mentioned that might be important during story development, but never got back to, etc. Good players will pick up on these items and they could cause a problem. Keep track of everything by writing your ideas down. Start writing down what props you may need to buy or create, such as a murder weapon, maps, diaries, etc.

This is also a good time to decide how you want to incorporate "player help" in the game. In other words, ways to avoid people getting bored and/or frustrated during the game. There are many forms of help that can be incorporated into the game and these are covered in more detail later. The typical form of help I use includes the use of "help tickets" I hide around, same as I do clues, but make the help tickets a little easier to find. If a player finds a ticket they can ask me a yes or no question about the game. This is also explained in more detail later and I highly suggest you incorporate it into the game. It also keeps you more involved and interacting with the players.

Generating Story Ideas

One of the things people always ask me is "Where did you come up with that?" One of the fun, and sometimes equally tough parts of designing your mystery, is to come up with the story for the plot, puzzles, motives etc. So, this chapter of the book will give you some ideas on how to brainstorm for your story.

Depending on the type of murder mystery you want will also determine where you should look for your ideas, so lets start with ghost story type of mysteries.

Existing ghost stories are the best place to start generating ideas for your murder mystery. Head to the library and take out a few ghost story books. You will have fun reading them and start formulating some ideas. Use the Internet. There are immeasurable stores of information that can be found on the Web. Rent some movies. One example of a movie with a good murder mystery ghost story was "Stir of Echoes". This movie had murderers and had a ghost that was trying to get in touch with the living to help bring her murderers to justice so that she could rest in peace.

This concept would be easy to turn into a murder mystery game. You can hide a 'body' someplace in your house, could be anywhere. You could even lock the body up and then the players would need to figure out the lock combination to get to the body. The victim could then be holding a crucial piece of evidence to identify the murder/murderers. There could be clues of all sorts 'left' by the ghost telling the story of what happened, giving hints of her whereabouts, and hints about how to go about getting the combination or key to open the door or trunk where she is.

Check into any local legends. These can range from hidden gold from the Civil War to money hidden and never found from a bank robbery. Maybe this gold or money is suspected to be on your property. The players could find the money and remains (Bones, Clothes, etc) of the previous person who tried to find the gold. The murderer is at the party to stop anyone else from finding the stash.

Check into the local history of your area. One of my murder mysteries was built around Indians that previously lived in my area. (See Sample Game Four) This was fun to do and a lot of the history about the Indians and the area was true. I just added in some gold and a curse. You can check for local ghost stories, those can be fun to change around a little to fit your story. Ask the long time residents in the neighborhood if they know of any. You never know what you will turn up.

Plenty of books also exist about real murder mysteries solved and unsolved. This is a more macabre way of generating ideas, but a way to give you ideas for plots nonetheless. Then there is always TV shows, movies, books, magazines: Edger Allen Poe, Alfred Hitchcock, Steven King, Nancy Drew mysteries and even Scooby Doo has some good mysteries which will help you generate ideas.

Murder Weapon and Body

The murder weapon you choose, as with everything else in the game, is open to your imagination. In Sample Game One, it was a fireplace poker. In Sample Game Two it was assault with bare hands, Sample Game Three was a phone, Sample Game Four was open for the imagination, but a decapitation was involved and Sample Game Five was zombification. As you can see, it really can be just about anything you want, poison, knife, gun, etc. If you get really creative, it can be things such as curses or even a 'Stare of death'. Whatever you choose, just make sure it fits into your story and you can explain its existence or non-existence within the game.

Along with accounting for a murder weapon, you are also going to have to account for a body (or bodies). The people are going to want to see the victim!

There are many ways to represent a murder victim and once again they all depend on your imagination and creativity. Here are five of my past victims and how they appeared at the party. All of these are explained better in the party samples in later chapters.

1) A stuffed dummy with a balloon head covered with a white tee shirt. As he was supposed to be alive at the start of the game, I drew a mean face with magic marker on the shirt. His 'head' was popped after the murder and fake blood splattered on the tee shirt.

2) A plastic skeleton that was really a Halloween decoration. It was actually flat, because I could not find a better one at the time, so in the story the murderer said he ran him over with a steamroller to make him easier to hide. Everyone got a kick out of that.

3) A jar with ashes and plastic costume teeth. The victim was cremated by the murderer, to try to hide the body.

4) A plastic skull. The rest of the body was found elsewhere and taken away by police.

5) The 'body' was actually a zombie that roamed the party scaring people and giving some hints. (This was one of the parties when I assigned this role to a person. As the party went on he added more zombie makeup to his face (decaying). It was fun when people finally figured out what was going on)

You can pretty much do whatever you like as far as a body is concerned. I even made a small wooden coffin one year that the players had to dig up and examine evidence in the coffin. Some evidence is all that is needed. Your imagination, once again, is your only limit as to what type of body you will have. The victim technically does not even have to be a human. Who is to say that a beloved pet hamster could not have been murdered?

Game Help

The help system of a game serves at least two purposes:
1) To actually help players.
2) To add another time control factor.
This can help speed up or slow down the pace of the game. This is great for preventing lulls, and I really suggest you integrate some kind of timing technique during the game. My usual help system is done by dispensing 'help' tickets. I use a role of red raffle type tickets. As I walk around watching over the party, I drop tickets on the floor, or I just hide them as I would clues. This ticket entitles the finder to ask me one yes or no question about the mystery: at my discretion, of course. So a question like "Is so and so the murderer?" will not be answered. But a question like "Is it worth my while to search the garden?" or "Is this symbol on this paper an important clue?" will be answered with a simple yes or no. This is a great way to help a game along. If your guests are having a tough time or are not making progress, start dropping more question tickets. During your briefing with your guests at the beginning of the night, tell them about these tickets so your players know to look out for them and what they are for. When a player approaches me with a question I will bring them to the side to avoid any other players from listening in.

There are other things that can be done as well along the same lines. For example, each person can ask five (or as many as you wish) questions, people can ask a question every 10 or 20 minutes, tell me one fact and you get two in return, etc. One important side note is to remember to give your murderer a bunch of help tickets, if you're using that type of system, during the briefing. This way during the party the murderer can come talk to you at any time. People will see the red ticket and not get suspicious, instead they will think the player (murderer) has just found the ticket.

Tips For Choosing Your Murderer

This is a very important part of your game design. First off, the person you choose should want to play the role. Don't choose someone who you think would rather be solving the game. Most people would like to do both, but there are a few that would rather be involved in the solving of the mystery instead of trying to thwart the attempts. Choose someone who can keep a secret well. It would not be too much fun if shortly after the game begins, your murder slips up and lets the cat out of the bag. This is another a good reason to have people not only figure out who the murderer is, but also figure out the details: why, how, when, etc. It is a nice way to add another dimension to the game instead of just trying to figure out, "Who did it".

Also keep in mind not to pick someone who is too good for the role. Don't pick someone in your group of friends who has always been known to be sneaky, lie, etc. These types of people are best left as regular players as they will most likely be the first ones accused, making them a good decoy. There is also no rule restricting you to one murderer. Partners in crime would be a fun game and most people would not even think of that.

To reiterate an earlier point, you always want to have a back up murderer, just in case your original does not show up, refuses to be a murderer, etc. Whenever I design the game I always make it possible to change whom the murderer is. In Sample Game One, it was simply a matter of changing who's absolution I did not distribute. In Sample Game Two, It was a matter of changing the stickers on the bones. All I had to do was write different letters on some more stickers and apply.

In Sample Game Three, I used the keys of a typewriter stuck in the depressed position to indicate some of the letters of the killer's name. The letters could have been changed by changing the depressed keys of the typewriter. Changing a number letter key is also an easy thing to do. If you are using a clue that yields a number which is suppose to associate with a letter, then it is easy to make that change. For example, instead of the players finding a key (decoder) that said, A = 4, B = 5, I would create a new one that says A = 9, B = 3, etc. I highly recommend that you take this into consideration when designing your game solution.

How the murderer should go about playing the game is something I would like to touch upon again. I like to give the people playing the role of the murderer free verse. They can pretty much do anything they want, other than destroy or modify clues, props, etc. The one condition is that I am aware what it is they are doing. This is one reason I give them help tickets, during any point in the game they can pull me over to the side and talk to me.

One other technique I use, is for the murderer to hide clues that they find in a specific place. I usually use a medicine cabinet or closet in a bathroom. I will have to change that now since my players will, I am sure, be reading this book! Simply choose a spot that is very hard to come across and that it would be difficult for someone to see what you are doing. Tell your murder to place clues that they find there every half-hour or so. I typically will keep checking every 45 minutes and take a look at what has been 'removed' from the game. I will redistribute the clues, puzzles, etc so the game can continue. If the murderer has done a very good job, been creative, etc, this is taken into account at the end of the game, since I usually determine a winner. If the murderer continually found clues that would otherwise make them undetectable, I will most likely say they have won the game, unless someone can prove they found that clue before the murderer did.

Difference Between Puzzles and Clues

Q: What is the difference between a puzzle and a clue?
A: A clue is an item that is needed to solve the murder mystery and a puzzle is what needs to be solved to obtain that clue.

Q: Do all clues need to be puzzles?
A: No, some clues can simply be found, read out of a book (which is used as a prop for the game), given at a certain time, etc. As a matter of fact there should be more clues than puzzles to make the game move along and for people to not get stuck with nothing happening in the game.

Once you have a solid story line, you can pull out key facts and use these as the clues that need to be found to solve the mystery. Then some of these clues can be turned into puzzles that must be solved in order to obtain the clue. Typically you will want to make the most important facts (what drove the story) the most difficult to obtain or figure out, making them into puzzles is a way to accomplish this.

I have included a diagram (see fig. 1) to visually represent the relationship between puzzles and clues. Notice the thicker line on the left, labeled story line, has a "Beginning" and an "End". Imagine this to be your story line. Now imagine taking out pieces of your story line, making the line discontinuous. You could never reach the end of the line with those pieces missing. Each of those pieces is a clue, and when the clues are placed back into the story line, you can reach the end. So as stated before, the clues can simply be important pieces of the story line, a time, place, name, letter, number, etc. Note: The figure is purely an example. Your murder mystery should contain many more clues and puzzles than represented in the figure.

Now for each of the removed pieces of the story line, which are now clues, you can decide how the players will obtain the clue. On the diagram I have added, 'placed' and 'puzzle'. A placed clue is simply the clue hidden someplace. It is the actual time, place, name, letter, number, etc that is missing from the story line. These are easy clues, since once found they reveal a part of the story line. The other type I have is a puzzle. These are puzzles that need to be solved before the clue can be revealed. These types of puzzles will be discussed on the next chapter; but they can be as simple as a riddle or even a word jumble. I have also indicated a double puzzle. This is a situation where a puzzle must be solved to reveal a clue. This clue in turn is needed to reveal the clue missing from the story line. For example, the players must first decode a number/letter key, which reveals the combination to a locked box which contains the last will and testament of Dr. Frankenstein. As you can see from the diagram, once you have your story line created, you simply need to pull out key facts and figure out how your players are going to go about obtaining them.

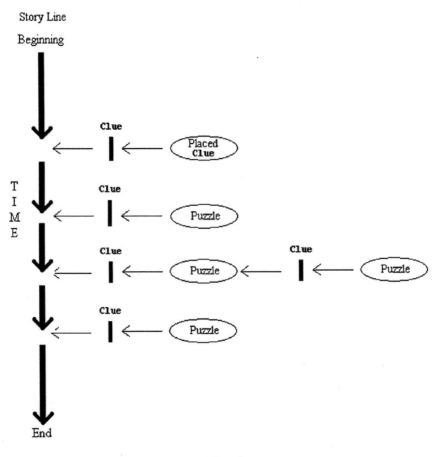

Fig. 1

Generating Ideas for Puzzles and Clues

Once you have a story line developed, you are going to need to pull it apart as Fig. 1 shows. Lets start out with clues. Clues are the easier of the two because these can simply be portions of the story line. The clues can be in many forms, paper, tape recordings, video, etc. The possibilities are endless.

In Sample Game One, the clues were easy, they were portions of the story line typed on pieces of paper and hidden around the house. Finding each clue gave more information about each of the players and their relationships to Brent. An additional clue was the pin that had to be found. For observant players, this was an important one.

In Sample Game Two, there were clues to find in the form of diary pages, pieces of a map that had to be pieced together to find the treasure, bones with initials, etc

Sample Game Three had many types of clues, from paper to microscopes to an actual recording the players could listen to.

As you can see, clues can come in many forms and are simply parts of your story.

Now you're going to need a few challenges for your players to solve. That's where puzzles come in. Besides supplying the players with the puzzles which will give them a clue in the form of information, locations, or hints needed to solve other puzzles, etc, puzzles can also help in the timing of the game. The more difficult a puzzle is the more time it will take to solve. But remember to keep a good balance as not to frustrate and bore your players.

There are endless types of puzzles that can be incorporated into your game. This is a great place to exercise your creativity. Just about anything can be made into a puzzle. As stated above, puzzles can be things as simple as a bit of the story line (clue) written down on a piece of paper and then the paper is torn into a number of pieces. The information is not very useful until all the pieces are found and matched together.

Some sources of ideas for puzzles are IQ books, riddle books, puzzle books, etc. The solutions of these puzzles can be modified to reveal a clue. You can set it up any which way you like. Maybe you need to solve two puzzles to figure out one clue. A simple example used in Sample Games Two, Three and Four is that solving a puzzle revealed a letter or a number. In the case where it reveals a number, this was checked against a number/letter key (decoder) that was also created.

18

This key, which can also be set up as another clue or clues (hide the key for example), will reveal the letter. Let's say your player solved a puzzle and the solution to this puzzle is the number 4. When he or she finds the key, it will say "A = 4". So if you have a key such as A = 4, S = 2 and M = 6, you can have them solve three separate number puzzles to reveal the three numbers 4,2,6. From this the players can construct the name SAM. The letter or number can be a clue and once the players have a number of clues, the players can try to piece together the word, which spells out the murderer's name.

One in particular that I like is the 'paper on paper puzzle/clue. In other words if you put a number of pieces of paper together and look at them through a light the papers together create a picture, name, number, etc. But when you have each paper individually it's not obvious what it's for. An example of this I used in Sample Game Four, and is shown in Fig. 2. I had three separate pieces of paper, on each sheet was a separate picture. First sheet shows a key and a hieroglyphics type image.

The second sheet shows a skull and a hieroglyphics type image, the third a C-clamp (represented with an arrow to indicate tightening of the clamp)
and a hieroglyphics image. If you lined up the pages by aligning the hieroglyphics image (which is the only common image between all three sheets) by combining the sheets and placing one on top of the other, the picture would now be a skull with a key in it being crushed by a C-clamp. This was what needed to be done to the plaster cast skull I made with a key in it. If the players found these clues and solved the 'puzzle', they would know what needed to be done to the skull and how.

Everyone has different talents; some people are good at woodworking, while some people are good at sewing. Whatever your talents are, try to incorporate it into the game. You can do this either directly, such as having a murder mystery based around your talent, or use your talent to make puzzles and clues. For example, if you're a good painter, you can base your murder mystery around a stolen painting. The artist might have suspected someone would try to steal their painting and that they were in danger. In the painting/paintings (the one you're going to paint), the painter included some clues as to who, what or where information might be found. Also, remember not to make any clues gender specific, that could make for a quick ending or at least halve

19

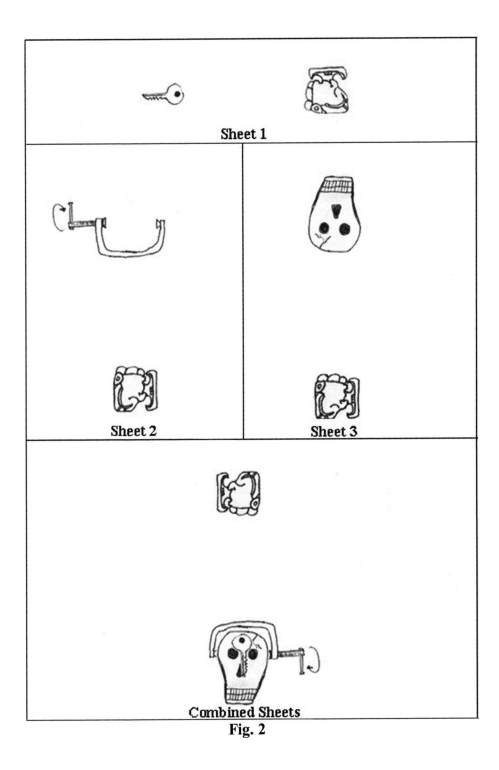

Sheet 1

Sheet 2

Sheet 3

Combined Sheets

Fig. 2

the time if you have a 50/50 ratio of male to female guests. If you like, you could always save a gender specific clue for the end, narrowing the field in the last minutes of the game, solidifying suspicions for some and forcing others to rethink theirs.

There are an infinite amount of options for clues and puzzles; use you imagination and you will come up will all kinds. I also like to pay attention to detail and help to set the mood with my clues and puzzles. For example, on some of the paper clues I will burn the edges of the paper, on some of the puzzles. I will try to make them look old, put some fake blood on them, etc. Anything that will help set the mood but stays consistent with my story line.

Timing

The timing of your game is important, it will determine a number of factors, including how long the game is suppose to last, how long you make it actually last and how much fun your players are having.

One simple technique to control the timing of a game is to limit the amount of clues the players can find at any given time. For example, let's say you have a total of fifty clues that need to be found to solve the mystery and reveal the murderer. Don't put out all fifty clues right away, as this might lead to a fast ending. Instead put out a few clues and then judge how the game is going. Pace your clues. Also, don't forget, that if you set the clues up properly, the players might be able to solve the mystery to the point of how the murder was committed and what the motive was, but still not know who did it.

If the players are having trouble, put out more clues. If players are figuring things out fast, wait a while. They will not know how many clues there are and will keep looking for more. You can easily pace a game this way.

Puzzle difficulty is another way to time a game. The harder the puzzles are, the longer it will take them to solve. This can be controlled using the help system you incorporate if things get too hard.

In an emergency situation you might need to think on your feet. If your party is suppose to last about three hours, but your guests have been able to solve some major puzzles in an hour, you only have five more clues to put out and no more puzzles to solve, this is a bad situation. Since you can't go back in time, your game is going to be shorter than planned. But since you have five clues left, see if you can half or even triple those clues somehow. If they are paper clues, just rip them in half. Be reasonable with this, don't make it too obvious and make sure you still keep the game moving.

One technique that I use to my advantage is party games. Since we have the murder mysteries during our annual Halloween party, we always have additional party games, such as apple bobbing, a piñata, pumpkin bowling, etc. I use these games to my advantage in two ways, one it gives me time to put out more clues, set things up, evaluate how things are going, etc.

Two, it gives everyone a break, while your players may not stop talking about the murder mystery, they are playing a different game, so it's a nice break. Sometimes I will even hide clues in the piñata or someplace else if the party game allows. Obviously you cannot be running the party games as well. Have someone else be in charge of the party games in order to free you up.

Another aspect you need to consider is how long to run a game. I design mine to run about three hours. This is never exact and depends on a number of factors, but typically between two and four hours is good, depending on the type of party and how many people are involved. If you're only having a dinner party with a few guests, then two hours might be a good target. If you're having a big party and the murder mystery is the main focus of the party, then maybe three or four hours depending on how many guests you have coming. The game can of course run as long as you wish, the thought has crossed my mind to have a weekend long murder mystery, where the players would have to go to different places to find clues. Maybe they need to explore the actual murder scene or interview neighbors if you can get them involved, etc.

Keeping People Involved

The main goal for your murder mystery should be for people to have fun. Keep your eyes open, not only for the game pace, but to make sure people are enjoying themselves. During the game, friends might group together really fast and things might get very secretive. If you have people at your party who don't know everyone or are shy, they might get left out and find themselves working alone. This could also be by choice, but it's best to find out. Talk to them and try to judge if they are trying to work alone, in which case they should have some clues they are keeping from people. If not, you need to help them mingle more. In most cases I will set it up that this particular person finds a major clue or even drop it at their feet. Remember the main goal is fun, so if someone seems bored or left out, I will bend the rules slightly to help them out. If I do this, then as I mingle around monitoring how things are going I will mention to a group that so and so has a good clue. It does not take long before they are invited to join that group. Another way to do this in advance is to know your guest's talents/abilities. Lets say you have a friend visiting from Germany who does not know anyone and is a little shy. Put out some clues in German, making sure you have worked that into the story line. This can be as simple as giving the murderer or victim a German parent, a past business trip to Germany, etc. This approach will encourage people getting together. People will need him or her to decipher that clue. This is fun to do and really personalizes the game.

Difficulty Level

Another factor that you need to take into consideration is how difficult you make the game. If people are not making any progress in the game, they will get frustrated and bored, which of course defeats the whole purpose of the game in the first place.

Keep in mind, as you are creating the game, that you know what is going on as far as story developments goes, know all the answers and how the players need to go about getting them. A game that seems easy to you may actually be difficult, and if the game seems difficult to you, then it is going to be very hard for the players.

The way to avoid this is to play the game yourself, not literally, but a mental run through. If there are physical puzzles that need to be solved, then yes, physically run through those to make sure they can be done. Also, be realistic. If, for instance, you are using Morse code to solve a puzzle, think about the following questions. Will people really know Morse code without having access to a decoder sheet? Will people even recognize Morse code, without it being mentioned someplace in the game? Try playing the game from scratch to see if you truly think your clues can be found, your puzzles solved, etc.

In summary, it is worthwhile to spend the time while designing to ensure your players are challenged, but not frustrated.

Game Ending

Once I see that that all or the majority of clues/puzzles have been found/solved, and the players seem like they have done all they can, I will give a 10 minute or so game ending warning.

Once the game has come to a close, I will gather everyone into a circle. I then pass out a piece of paper and pencil to everyone there and tell them to write down all they know about the murder, the murderer, the story line, etc, including their name on the paper. Basically, the players need to ask themselves, who, what, where, when, why, etc. If there were any special questions that might have come up, I will tell the players to answer those as well. An example is in Sample Game Three, "Is Mr. Greinder dead or alive? Where is he or his body?" I only give players about five minutes to write down their conclusions, so they are not writing too much.

Once time is up, I collect all the papers and begin reading them aloud. This usually leads to a number of laughs and is good fun. Once I have read through all the papers, I ask the murderer to stand up. Some people will not be surprised, others will. Since I give out prizes, I usually give out first, second and third, so even if the murderer has gone undetected, I will give prizes to those with the closest answers.

That's it; your game is now over and will be engrained in people's memories for a long time.

MURDER AT 903 HELENA DRIVE
Sample Game One

This first sample murder mystery is the easiest of the five and is actually the first one that I created. It is easy to set up, cheap to create and the only knowledge you need is a motive for 'murder' for each one of your guests. Lets just jump right in and you will see what I mean.

Set up (prior to party):

First thing you will need for this murder mystery is a murder victim. For this all you need is a representation of a person. I made a dummy. I used an old pair of jeans and a button down shirt, sewed them together, stuffed them with rags and gave him a balloon head covered with a white tee shirt. On the tee shirt I drew a mean looking face. He did not have any hands or feet, but looked good enough. You can do something similar or use any type of scarecrow type of entity, even a card board cut out would work, but might not be as much fun. Now you must give him a name. I used Brent Mueller. From this point on I will refer to him as Brent.

The next step will take a little thinking. Write down all the guests that will be coming to the party, and, next to each, something individual to them, their job, hobbies, habits, etc.

Now, for each of your guests you must think of something that Brent has 'said' that will make them 'mad'. Now remember this is to be fun, don't think of anything that will really anger someone or hurt his or her feelings. We had a number of people from all walks of life coming to the party, A bowling alley employee, residents of Columbus Ohio, a speech therapist, a couple getting married on Christmas day, and many many more. These examples were all characteristics about these people that were individual to them. So if I had two speech therapists coming, I could not use that. Each item has to specific to only one person or a couple at most. So now I wrote down some things that would give them a motive.

"Brent was heard earlier this evening stating "Columbus Ohio should be leveled to make room for industry"

"Brent was heard earlier this evening stating "That anyone who works in a bowling alley should be shot"

"Brent was heard earlier this evening stating "Any marriages performed on Christmas day should not be recognized"

"Brent was heard earlier this evening stating "Speech therapy is a wasted career"

I think you get the idea. Brent is just a very rude guy and has said something to make everyone really really mad.

The next step is to write down counters for all his insults.

"After being shown a bunch of pictures of Columbus Ohio, Brent decides it's beautiful and is going to buy a house in the area.

"After admitting to bowling a couple of frames, Brent admits he truly loves the game"

"After speaking with people at the party, Brent has decided that marriages on Christmas are a great thing. He even stated he would be willing to pay for one"

"After being cured of his lisp at the party, Brent offered the speech therapist the top position a the newly formed 'Brent Mueller Speech Therapy school, paying $300,000 per year.

As you can see, all the bad things Brent has said have now been absolved. This is fun and a little silly, but it helps everyone get to know each other, will make them mingle and everyone will have some laughs.

You need to create absolutions for everyone at the party. The night of the party you can choose who will be the murderer and don't distribute their absolution sheet. That person will be the only one with whom Brent has not made peace.

One of the other props you will need prior to the party is a small pin, necklace or some <u>small</u> piece of jewelry. Since our party was a Halloween party, I picked up a small Halloween pin. It was a little mummy.

I always create an introduction/rule sheet to hand out to everyone, I use it to set up the story and to explain the rules of the game.

Here is a copy of my Intro:

WELCOME TO MURDER AT 903 HELENA DRIVE

One of the people at this party will be murdered this evening. You must find out who did it and why. At the end of the evening the person who can solve the crime with the most proof will be the 'winner'. Everyone at the party knows something different and speaking to as many people as you can will be very helpful. Throughout the party you should be aware of hints lying about. These will most likely take the form of a piece of paper with a sentence or two written on it. You can share, trade or keep this information for yourself. There may be valuable hints that you will have to find yourself. Hints will be restricted to the basement, living room, kitchen and outside the house. Enjoy...

Introducing Brent Mueller

If you have not already met Brent, he is the cocky-looking gentleman dressed in jeans a flannel shirt and baseball cap. He is in need of a tan. Brent was born in Berlin Germany, 1955. He was an abused child that swore revenge on the world. At the age of eighteen he left his parents and came to the U.S, vowing to become rich and famous. By the age of 25 he was a millionaire. His success can be attributed to lying, cheating and stealing. In 1981 both his parents disappeared without a trace. The case has never been solved. In 1985 he was granted a U.S. citizenship and is very proud of it.
Today Brent is a multibillionaire, building contractor, land developer and influential politician with connections in all the right places. It has been said, to have Brent Mueller on your side is better than a guaranteed ticket to heaven. On the darker side, it is often said that when Brent Mueller wants something he gets it and the only way to stop him would be to kill him.

Brent was heard earlier this evening stating "Columbus Ohio should be leveled to make room for industry"

The final sentence in the intro/rules handout is one of the motives you created earlier. You will need to make enough copies to hand out to everyone and everyone's copy will have a different motive as the last sentence. When you're handing out the Intro, make sure you do not give the motive for whom it was created. For example, you have an Architect coming to the party, Brent mentioned that he could do a better job designing any building any time than any architect. Do not give the Intro sheet with that motive on it to the architect. This will encourage people to talk to each other and find out who is the architect. It will also give people the opportunity to lie about themselves if they so choose, but either way people will be socializing.

<u>The night of the party</u>
Have your dummy set up before people start arriving. For my party I had Brent sitting at a table with a bottle of Absolute Vodka next to him. As people came in I would introduce him as if he was a real person at the party.

Once all your guests have arrived, determine, if you have not already, who your murderer will be and remember not to distribute that person's absolution with Brent's peacemaking sentence on it. That is the only person who will still have a motive at the end of the night.

Next, set yourself up someplace where you cannot be heard and begin calling people in and give them their briefing. When the murderer comes in, tell them that their role is to basically lie if they can get away with it, and try to find clues before others do. Try not to get to specific, let them be creative and see what they come up with. Just tell him/her they cannot destroy anything or ruin a clue. What I will do sometimes is I will tell the murderer to hold on to the clues they find and then every half hour or so put them in a predetermined place, for example, a bathroom closet. I will check every hour or so, and recycle the clues they have found, giving them credit for those clues. If the murderer keeps finding major clues, that basically would make them undetectable if I did not recycle the clues they found, at the end of the party they will either win or get some kind of prize.

Have the murderer wear the pin or small jewelry item I mentioned. Make it visible, but not obvious. This will be a clue left near the body after the murder.

During this part, people can start talking right after they have been briefed - clues have not been put out, so there is nothing to find. They can begin talking to each other and try to figure out who matches the motive the received.

After all of your guests have been briefed, they all should be chatting and comparing notes. People should start finding out about the bad things Brent has said about them. Once your guests have had some time to chat, your going to need to distract them so you can begin planting clues. As stated previously we did this during a Halloween party so the first party game was apple bobbing and everyone went outside. You can do the same thing or just tell them not to go down the basement for a while, or wherever you are going to start planting clues. How you distract them is up to you. When your players are outside or otherwise distracted, place a few of the absolution clues around. Hide them in places where you don't care if people look. I would put them in places with half the paper sticking out. For instance: in-between books, under pots, etc. Then let them just wander back in or announce new clues are out, which ever you choose. At the same time you can place some of the red tickets around as well, the ones they can use to ask a yes or no question. Once the first clue is found, people will know what to look for and the game will start picking up. After about 20 minutes we started another party game, it was a piñata which we were going to break in the basement. I had told the murderer that when we started this game to go to the bathroom and leave the mummy pin in the closet. While everyone was downstairs wrecking the basement trying to break a piñata, I carried Brent outside, popped his balloon head and spread fake theatrical blood on the white tee shirt that was his head. The fake blood was the type you can always find around Halloween. I placed one of the fireplace pokers near him, hence the murder weapon. Hold onto the mummy pin for now as it is a great piece of evidence and we don't want to give out a game-ending clue right in the beginning of the game. We are going to hide the mummy pin later and say, "It must have fallen off during the struggle". I was very interested to see if anyone who found it would have been observant enough to remember who was wearing that pin. I also hid some more of the 'making peace' clues around. Make sure your assistant (if you have one) keeps your guests away from you during this time. For me it was just a matter of keeping the guests down the basement. Once the stage was set and I knew the piñata was broken, I yelled down to the guests, "Oh My god, someone has killed Brent." They come running up the stairs as if it was a real person, pretty funny.

At this point I let them examine the crime scene. I hid an absolution clue in Brent's pocket for the person who thought of searching the body. That person will usually just about get tackled to the ground when they see he or she pull out a clue from the pocket.

From this point on just let the game flow on its own. The guests should be trying to find out information about each other, trading clues, looking for more clues, trying to figure out who would have a motive, etc. People will also start reaching for any clue to who the murderer is as well. One funny instance of this was when my wife asked one of my friends to help bring in a cooler. At the end of the game when I was reading out everyone's "who was the murderer and why" reports, someone said that the murderer must have been the person bringing in the cooler. The player came up with this because they believed the person asked to bring in the cooler was being forced into manual labor and was angry at the world. The player making the accusation did not find or get the information proving that the 'cooler carrier' had absolution with Brent.

As the night moves forward, position yourself alone outside near the murder scene or do it during another party game while everyone is preoccupied. Be careful, people will catch on and someone might try to sneak out and see what you are up to. At this point, hide the pin someplace near the body. I put it in some grass about four feet away. Now you can say to everyone that they did not search the crime scene well enough and people will charge outside looking around, or you can tell that to the next person to give you a red ticket, etc, etc.

I had to hint around a little for my players to find it. Remind them to keep it to themselves if they remember who was wearing it. Sometimes in their excitement players will yell something out and give away the information. They might have been the only person observant enough to remember who had on the pin, so they don't want to give it away. It is also up to them if they want to share what they or their team has found. In my case no one was observant enough to remember who was wearing the pin. Once I saw the game was slowing down and there were no more clues to be found, I announced the game was over and asked everyone to write down on a piece of paper who the murderer was and why. Give everyone a few minutes and then have everyone sit around and you read them off. This always leads to lots of laughs. Once you are finished, ask the murderer to stand up, step forward, etc. Wait while everyone yells "I knew it!", "It was you?" "I cant believe it" "No way!!" etc. Then announce the winner, if you are playing that option.

That's it, your first custom-made murder mystery goes down in history and people will be talking about it for a while, and anxiously waiting for what you do next year.

32

Quick Game

This is the quick game set up. I am putting this here now since this game is a customized version of Sample Game One. Follow these simple directions and add in your own ideas. Have fun.

Step 1:

The title of your mystery can be as follow:

MURDER AT (Your Address Here)

Step 2:

First thing you will need for this murder mystery is a murder victim. For this all you need is a representation of a person. For a dummy you can use an old pair of jeans and a button down shirt, sew them together, stuff them with rags and give him or her a balloon head covered with a white tee shirt. On the tee shirt draw a mean looking face. You can do something similar or use any type of scarecrow type of entity; even a cardboard cut out would work. During Halloween, stores sell all sorts of characters you can purchase for decorations, any of these could work, shop around. Give him or her a name.

Step 3:

The next step will take a little thinking. Write down all the guests that will be coming to the party, and, next to each, something individual to them, their job, hobbies, habits, etc.

Now, for each of your guests you must think of something that your 'dummy' has 'said' that will make them 'mad'. Now remember this is to be fun, don't think of anything that will really anger someone or hurt his or her feelings. If you have not already, check into some of the examples in game one. This is what will be giving everyone at the party an excuse to want to kill your 'dummy'.

Step 4:

The next step is to write down counters for you 'dummies' insults. In other words, something that your 'dummy' can say to make the particular guest he had insulted feel better. This is to eliminate people from wanting to kill your 'dummy'. See examples in game one.

Step 5:

You can add in the option of a visual clue, such as the pin mentioned in game one. Hold onto this until you decide who will be the murderer.

Step 6:

During this next step you need to create an introduction and rule sheet for the game. It can vary depending on which parts of the house you want to have off limits. The one that follows is just about the same one that is in game one. Brent Mueller was the name of my dummy in the game. You can change it and any of the information, such as age, place of birth, etc. I have left the *Introducing Brent Mueller* portion of the introduction for ease of reading, but feel free to change it.

WELCOME TO MURDER AT (Your Address Here)

One of the people at this party will be murdered this evening. You must find out who did it and why. At the end of the evening the person who can solve the crime with the most proof will be the 'winner'. Everyone at the party knows something different and speaking to as many people as you can, will be very helpful. Throughout the party you should be aware of hints lying about. These will most likely take the form of a piece of paper with a sentence or two written on it. You can share, trade or keep this information for yourself. There may be valuable hints that you will have to find yourself. Hints will be restricted to (choose the areas the player will be allowed to search). Enjoy...

Introducing Brent Mueller

If you have not already met Brent, he is the cocky-looking gentleman dressed in jeans a flannel shirt and baseball cap. He is in need of a tan. Brent was born in Berlin Germany, 1955. He was an abused child that swore revenge on the world. At the age of eighteen he left his parents and came to the U.S, vowing to become rich and famous. By the age of 25 he was a millionaire. His success can be attributed to lying, cheating and stealing. In 1981 both his parents disappeared without a trace. The case has never been solved. In 1985 he was granted a U.S. citizenship and is very proud of it.
Today Brent is a multibillionaire, building contractor, land developer and influential politician with connections in all the right places. It has

been said, to have Brent Mueller on your side is better than a guaranteed ticket to heaven. On the darker side, it is often said that when Brent Mueller wants something he gets it and the only way to stop him would be to kill him.

Brent was heard earlier this evening stating, "Columbus Ohio should be leveled to make room for industry"

The final sentence in the intro/rules handout is one of the motives you created earlier. You will need to make enough copies to hand out to everyone and everyone's copy will have a different motive as the last sentence. When you're handing out the Intro, make sure you do not give the motive to the person about whom it was created. For example, you have an Architect coming to the party, Brent mentioned that he could do a better job designing a building than any architect. Do not give the Intro sheet with that motive to the architect. This will encourage people to talk to each other and find out who is the architect, it will also give people the opportunity to lie about themselves if they so choose, but either way people will be socializing.

From this point on you should see that this is flowing exactly the same way as Sample Game One. The night of the party can flow the same way as page 23.

Use some creativity and you will have a game to be enjoyed and remembered.

DEAR UNCLE JAKE
Sample Game Two

Since the first year was such a success, I put more time and thought into the second year. I wanted to give the game a more spooky air about it since it was Halloween. I wanted the players to get pulled into a totally fictional scenario. I also wanted to try creating the whole story from scratch, and adding some new aspects to the game. In the end it worked out better than I expected, the people really were pulled into the story. This game had a story to follow, physical clues to find, piece together and, best of all buried treasure.

The motive behind this murder mystery was money. I created the story in the form of a diary. Lets start out with the story and diary:

11/09/97

Dear Diary,

Again I went to Uncle Jake's house. He is so old and fragile. The house is a huge old house. It is practically abandoned. He only uses the first floor living room, bathroom and kitchen. I gave him his food, by spoon again of course. He had one of his coughing fits again. I thought it was all over. His face gets beet red and he starts drooling. He caught his breath again and it was fine. He has no one but me to take care of him. I have to admit, knowing he has no one to leave all his money to but me is most likely why I am over here day after day taking care of the old man.

11/11/97

Dear Diary,

Uncle Jake was very nice to me today. He is actually great to talk to. He told me today that he is so happy and thankful that I have been able to take care of him since Aunt Carol passed away. We talk about him being in the 381st paratrooper group and some of his experiences in the war.

11/15/97

Dear Diary,

Today Uncle said something that has me worried. He mentioned something about leaving his money to a charity. I must have heard him wrong, but don't know how to bring it up without sounding too greedy. I had a few hours to kill today so I decided to stay a while at Uncles house. I started to explore the house a little. I had not been up to some of those rooms since I was a little kid. Everything seems untouched. As if time just stopped when Aunt Carol died.

11/19/97

Dear Diary,

Did some more exploring today. Found some of my old toys up in the attic. I don't even remember some of them. Found some old pictures of Uncle from the paratrooper days. He is getting sicker. I hate having to help him in the bathroom.

11/24/97

Dear Diary,

God I am really getting sick of taking care of him, he is driving me crazy. Coughing, gagging I am tired of it. Sometimes I think he would be better off dead. I found some old papers in an old desk drawer. Seems Uncle has more money stashed away than I thought. I also found some papers about Aunt Carol. Some organizations she belonged to and some seem like they would still be active; the dates are pretty current.

12/2/97

Dear Diary,
Well that does it, today that old bastard told me he was leaving all his money to one of Aunt Carols organizations. Some crap about children or dogs or something like that. I had asked him about Aunt Carol, just

to pass some time and then he throws that in. I can't believe it. I have been taking care of him all these years, dealing with the coughing and the spoon feeding and all the other crap. Now I come to find out that he is going to give it to charity. Maybe if I don't show up for a couple of days he will begin to see how important I am. He does not know I am upset, so I will give that a try.

12/5/97

Dear Diary,

Passed by the house today and saw uncle looking out the window waiting for me. He was not able to see me though. He had such a look of worry on his face, I think he was actually worried something happened to me.

12/13/97

Dear Diary,

Well that showed him. I come in the house, and there he is on the floor. Seems he fell two days ago and could not get up. He has had nothing to eat or drink since then. I should feel bad, but I don't. I deserve that money and he will soon realize it.

12/19/97

Dear Diary,

Uncle Jake thanked me a million times for coming to help him. I guess he realized how much he does need me. I pretended I was too busy with work and school to stop by. He said he is proud of me and to keep up the good work. I threw in how tough it is to work and go to school at the same time, maybe that will give him the hint.

12/21/97

Dear Diary,

Man, today he told me he is thinking about hiring a full time nurse. He said he felt bad that my schoolwork may be suffering because I come by here to help him. This is not good. I told him it was no problem. It is the money that makes it tough. Told him without our meetings, my life would be missing a big piece, hope that worked.

12/23/97

Dear Diary,

*Crap, Crap Crap!!! Did a real search of the house today. Found all sorts of papers. Seems once Uncle Jake dies, all his money will automatically get transferred to the Charities bank account.
Even if the money is not in the bank and a death certificate is registered they have legal right to the money. It is all signed and ready to go. There is no way for me to get the money. Unless...*

12/29/97

Dear Diary,

Well it worked, I told uncle that when the time comes, as this year's Christmas present, I promise to personally hand the money over to the charity and on that same day I will sprinkle his ashes over the grounds of the charities garden. He was overjoyed. He said he was so happy that a family member will present the money instead of a computer transaction. He is going to pull the money out of the bank in January to get the last interest on it.

1/2/98

Dear Diary,

Went to the bank with Uncle Jake today. His eyes lit up when we got outside. Seems he has not been out of the house for over two years. He looked like a kid when he sees a new toy. He has such a large amount of money that he hired one of the bank security guards to bring it by the house tomorrow, it would have been too much for us to carry.

1/4/98

Dear Diary,

Well that's that, the money is now in the house in a nice big chest. Now if I can figure out a way to prevent a death certificate from being registered I got it made. I think I will take some of the money and have a little fun. Just a few days worth.

1/18/98

Dear Diary,

Man, what a great time. I stayed in Europe much longer than I expected. Had a super time though. Met a girl named Heidi and a girl named Nicole. They were the best part. I guess I will go see Uncle Jake soon.

1/20/98

Dear Diary,

Oh My God, Oh My God. I don't know what to do. I did not mean it. He was yelling and screaming at me. He found out I took some money. He was screaming and yelling. He would not stop. I just meant to push him away from me. I guess I was too angry because I shoved him across the room and over a chair. His head hit the floor. I ran over to look just as the blood spilled from a huge wound. He looked at me for that last moment with shock. He grabbed my hand and held it, then he just stopped breathing. I ran from the house, what am I going to do?

1/20/98
Dear Diary,

I went back to the house again. There he is, eyes clouded over, color gone from his face. Just lifeless. I touched him and he was cold. What the hell am I going to do? If I call someone he will be declared dead then there goes the money and I go to jail. How could he do this to me?

40

1/22/98

Dear Diary,

How could he get so angry, I only took $10,000 dollars, that is nothing compared to what he has. He is just a greedy angry old man. I guess he deserved it otherwise it would not have happened.

1/25/98

Dear Diary,

As I went back to the house again, one of the neighbors stopped me and asked me what the smell was coming out of the back door. I told her there have been some troubles with the toilet, it must have over flowed again. The house stunk, he was all swollen and a black green color.

1/25/98

Dear Diary,

Went back again today with my bag and took out my tools. Talk about being a pain in the ass, he is dead and still giving me trouble. I tried just about every knife in the bag, it just was hell trying to cut through those old tendons and bones. Man I am pissed. I wasted the whole damn day. Tomorrow, I will have him in pieces.

1/26/98

Dear Diary,

The axe worked great, a chop here, a chop there, everywhere a chop chop. Ok, that's done. Now I need to stash Uncle Jake away for safe keeping, hide the loot for a while and wait till this blows over. I will say he is missing and that will give me plenty of time to figure out what to do. By the time they assume he is dead, me and the money will be long gone.

2/2/98

Dear Diary,

Old Uncle Jake was really smelling up the house. They are doing construction across the street from my house and they have a steamroller. I took Uncle Jake out there last night a tried to squish him. He flattened out all right, but he still stinks. With his bones nice and flat now he should be easier to hide.

2/8/98

Dear Diary,

Spent some time at the police station filling out the missing persons report. Still have uncle Jake at my place, have to find someplace for him soon.

2/12/98

Dear Diary,

Perfect. Today I went over a friends' house. While everyone was shooting the bull I took Uncle Jake out of the trunk and hid him all around the house. Some outside, some inside. By the time anyone finds the parts all that will be left are bones. One problem. In my boredom and my anger towards Uncle Jake for being such a pain I carved my name into some of his bones. For all eternity he will carry my name with him and know I have his money because he was such a pain. I doubt anyone could ever match me with the name. It just wont happen.

2/20/98

Dear Diary,

Today we were back over the same friends' house. This time I buried the money. I have a nice map so I can find it when the time comes. They have no clue about the body or the money.

5/30/98

Dear Diary,

Life has been boring since the Uncle Jake days. Everyone is looking for him. No family or anything, just the neighbors think he is wandering the streets or something. I need a vacation from all these nutty people. Went to a cookout at the house recently, everything is fine, they have no clue at all.

6/23/98

Dear Diary,

People from the newspaper came here today about Uncle Jake. I told them how I was taking care of him and that I came over one day and the door was open. I looked around for him and he was no where to be found. After the camera was off the reporter hugged me and told me everything would be fine. I knew that was true already.

8/11/98

Dear Diary,
Just got back from three weeks in Hawaii. I snuck by the house and got some of the money. Just enough for the three weeks. It has been a while. It could seem like I have been saving it all this time. It should be ok.

8/28/98

Dear Diary,

Bought some books on starting my own business, this should help me in the future if people start asking questions about the money. I have everything under control.

9/5/98

Dear Diary,

Picked up some more money the other night. Went to Vegas and lost a load. Plenty where that came from.

10/30/98

Dear Diary,

DAMN!!!!!!!!!! Problems, big Problems. Tomorrow night they're having a big Halloween party at the house. They are doing some kind of murder mystery crap. How corny can you get. This is a problem, they will be poking around the house all night looking for their little clues. They might stumble across the money or the body parts. I will be at the party and will do all I can to stop them from finding anything out.

10/30/98

Dear Diary,

I have decided to get rid of the map. First I tore it up and started to burn it but realized I could forget where I hid the money. I instead hid the pieces in places around the house. When the party is over I will pick them up.

10/31/98

Dear Diary,

Well here I am. Party is not bad so far. The hosts of the party, Joe and Sara, I think their names are, are really the best. I will mingle and pretend to be involved in this silly game. I am sorry to say Diary that I must also be rid of you. If by some chance I am caught and they find this Diary on me or in my house I am obviously in trouble. I have set up a flawless system that will automatically burn this book to a crisp. Fair well trusty diary.

The basic premise used here, and that has been used time and time again, is a murder to get an inheritance. Each Diary entry is a hint and was a separate piece of paper. I tried not to give too much information in each hint and I also did some emotion change in a few of them. Sometimes it seems like he likes his Uncle, other times it seems like he hates him. Then there is Aunt Carol, is she involved some how? I could not find the exact skeleton prop I was looking for, all I was able to find was a plastic flat skeleton that is suppose to hang on a door or wall, hence that addition of diary entry 2/2/98. I also tried to make it seem real by entries 2/12/98, 2/20/98, 8/11/98, 10/30/98, and 10/31/98. This is always fun to add.

Prior to the start of the party I hid all the bones around the outside of the house. I used stickers on the bones to represent the carved letters of the killer. Just in case the chosen murderer did not show, I could replace the stickers. The skeleton I bought broke up into ten separate pieces. The person whose name I used that year had only 5 letters, so some of the bones were blank. Even once the players had all the bones they would still have to put them all together to figure out whose name the letters spelled. I hid the bones fairly well so no one would find the bones unless the players were really looking and the players would not be looking unless they found the diary entry for 2/12/98. A few days before the party I buried the 'treasure', a bag of pennies, in the yard as well. I did it a few days before so the ground did not look freshly dug. Since it was fall, there was some time for more leaves to fall and cover it up. The players would not know about the treasure unless they found entry 2/20/98 and then would only know where to dig by finding the map! I tore the map into several pieces, so the players would have to assemble the pieces before they could find out exactly where the treasure was. For dramatic effect, I burned all of the edges of the diary pieces. This took a while, but it looked really good and added to the whole effect. Only burn the outer edge of the entire map, otherwise it will be harder to put together, unless you want to make it that difficult.

The map was done on my computer using Microsoft Paint brush, nothing fancy, but did the trick.

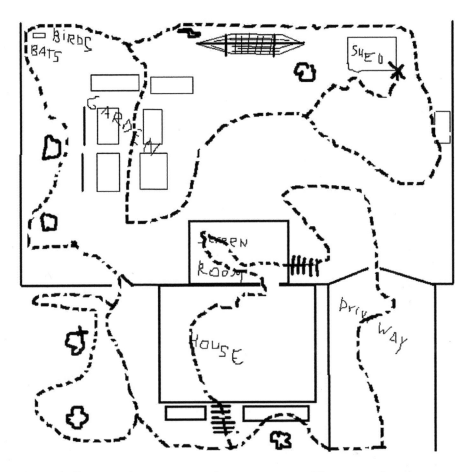

The path lines on the map served two purposes. First, was that every piece of the map they found had a portion of the path on it, this was to avoid them trying to zero in on it and digging at random. The second was that if they followed the paths they would find clues along it.

During this party I handed out envelopes; it made the whole briefing procedure faster. In each envelope was a rule sheet and in some of them I also included a diary entry. I did this randomly, and it forced people to start talking right away to see who got what. Here is the rule sheet I used this year:

RULES/HINTS

1. The game takes place in the following areas:
  Outside, the entire grounds is involved in the game.
  Living room
  Kitchen
  Dinning room
  All other rooms (bedrooms, upstairs bathroom, closets, etc) are not in the game.
  Basement. The main part of the basement is in the game. There is nothing on or behind the large wooden bench. Items will not be placed in boxes, so no need to waste time looking there. To find clues, nothing will need to be disassembled.

2. If you find a red ticket, you are entitled to a hint. See me to cash in your ticket.

3. If you think you need an item, or are going to do something on the grounds, ask me first. This may help you and/or stop you from wasting your time or giving others hints by your actions.

4. Enjoy and good luck!!

The Murderer got a rule sheet, some red help tickets and the additional sheet below, meant to look like another diary entry from the back, same pattern, burned edges, etc. Always give the murderer everything you give your other players, people might ask to see something, and if they do not have it, suspicions will fly. This year had a little more detail involved:

Well, guess what! You are the killer. The object of the game for you is lie, lie, lie. You have killed your Uncle for his inheritance, buried the loot in the back yard and hid his bones around the house. His bones are flat, you ran them over with a steamroller (Long Story). You also etched letters from your last name on the bones. No one has any clue about any of this yet. Everyone has been given a different page from your diary in their envelopes. Pieces of a map showing the buried loot are floating around the house. If they can match up some of the diary pages, they will get the story. If they find all the pieces of the map, they will find your loot, and if they find all the bones, they have your last name. I have given you a page from your diary so you can 'fit in' with everyone else. I would hide this paper fast. I also gave you a few of the red tickets, this way you can ask me questions without anyone getting suspicious. If you do have any questions, wait a while for the game to start spinning up. If anyone asks were you got the tickets, say you found them. You can think of a place. Remember, try to keep them off track without letting on your the killer. If they don't figure out it is you, you win. Good luck.

I also had Brent Muller still in the basement from last year, so I sat him up in a chair outside and put this in his pocket for someone to find:

Hi, If you don't recognize me, I am Brent Mueller. I was last year's murderee. My head has been repaired and I now I suffer eternally as a grappling dummy. I really have no major clues about this year's murder. I am just relaxing out here enjoying the night. But what I can tell you is that the killer is [I tore the paper off at this point]

This party was a great success. Everyone got caught up in the story. When the players dug up the treasure they where acting like they were expecting to find real gold. Everyone also got really caught up in the diary. The players all sat around and read it out loud at the end of the night. The Murderer won this game. He did a great job, his girlfriend of five years was surprised it was him, and that he was able to keep it a secret. He even hid some of the bones in his jacket.

One puzzle that I used during the party was given to me a while back. It was a maze type puzzle (see figure on next page). You put a bill in it, weather it be a dollar or a twenty, and have to maneuver a metal ball around a maze. Once you get it to the right spot, you can push a button and the drawer opens. Instead of a bill, I used clue, it was a nice additional puzzle for the players to solve.

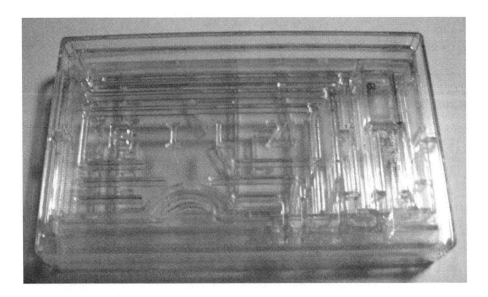

THE TALE OF MR. GREINDER
Sample Game Three

This party got bumped up several notches on the creative and preparation scale. I wanted to make this year a little scary and once again, have a different assortment of puzzles and clues. I also wanted to try my hand at creating a ghost story of sorts. It not really a ghost story about a ghost, but more of a story about trying to scare people away, your typical Scooby Doo type of mystery.

First let's start out with the story line I created:

Falls Church Ghost Stories

The Tale of Mr. Greinder

Strathmore Street was always a quiet area. Friendly neighbors, quiet weekends, the type of place to raise a family. This all changed on March 14th 1952, at least according to some folks.
William Coran was ten years old at the time and he still remembers when Mr. Greinder moved in. "We could never see his face, he was always looking down and would wear a hooded black jacket, even in the summer, we could never see his face. Some times at night I would look out my window and there he would be, staring right at me from the shadows of his house. Sometimes late at night I could feel him watching me through the walls. We would rarely see him during the day, and the house was almost always dark. At night is was a different story."
Wendy Luner was only eight and she can remember strange sounds and lights coming from the basement windows. "I was very young at the time, but we were all out playing ball one night after a family BBQ. The ball flew over our fence and rolled a ways into the driveway of the house. I was dared to go get it and gave in. As I neared the window where the ball was, I could see some lights in the window, really strange colors and the lights were getting dimmer and brighter very slowly. Just as I was about to grab the ball I heard a noise, no, it was more like a voice. All the hair stood up on my body as I had the feeling the voice was talking to me, asking me for help, whispering to me. I ran without taking the ball. I had nightmares for two months after that."

50

"We would tell our parents about this and would always be told that our imagination was running away with us, but we knew they were just as afraid as us" says Tom Redny. "We were about fifteen when we decided we were going to find out once and for all what was going on in that house. One October night we all climbed over the fence into the yard. It was me, Sam and Ben. The yard really did not look spooky in the day time, but at night it had lots of shadows. In the back of the yard was an old hammock, looked barely used. As the cool October air was blowing, the hammock started to swing slightly. We figured it was just the wind until we noticed the depression in the hammock was coming up as if someone was getting out of the hammock. We ran like hell, Ben swears he saw a face in the window of the shed as he looked back after hopping the fence. Sam hopped back over as fast and I ran towards the house for some reason. As I ran I could swear I felt hands grabbing at my legs trying to trip me. I got to the driveway and ran into the street and straight to my house, never looking back.

People will tell you all kinds of stories about the house and what went on there and things they say they have heard and seen. Even the neighborhood mailman was scared of the house. He said he delivered one letter to that house in all the years he worked the neighborhood. The children have grown and moved on, some even have had their own children. Most have not spoken about the house until this interview. The people who live in the neighborhood now say that about four years ago the house just 'died' no activity at all. No one has seen Mr. Griender lurking around. The house just sits there getting older. There was a claim by an older gentleman that has since passed on that he saw some people coming around the house, but then that suddenly stopped. No one knows what was really going on in that house. Some say he was a modern day Dr. Frankenstein trying to bring back his dead wife. Others say he was a warlock and was trying to communicate with spirits from beyond the grave. I guess we may never know...

What I did this year was turn my basement, or at least a portion of it into an abandoned lab. I will explain more later, but for now the story above was given to all the players as well as the following rules sheet:

How To Play

Sara and I have just moved into this house. We got a really good deal on it because of some ghost stories or something that has to do with the house. The only area that we have not ventured into yet is the basement. Tonight with your help, we will finally be venturing down there. Here's how the game will work.

1) People's names will be drawn from a hat, when your name is drawn you will have fifteen minutes to explore the basement, I will time you and call you when your time is up. You will get more than one chance to explore, so don't worry.

2) Your light source for the basement will be a lantern. It gets VERY hot so only hold it by the handle. Do not try to adjust the flame, it is as high as it can be right now without generating soot and smoking up the basement. Most importantly, always keep the lantern in front of you. If you need to put it down to look at something then always have it close where you can see it. This is for fire prevention.

3) As you descend the stairs, be careful and watch your footing.

4) Once you are at the base of the stairs, you will see the room is roped off with yellow and orange tape. DO NOT go outside the tape, stay within the boundaries. No matter what you hear, feel or see, do not go outside the tape.

5) There are many things to look at, solve, work, etc. Do whatever you like except don't break anything. There are things that you might have to assemble to get to work.

6) Whatever you move, assemble, use, etc return it back to the way you found it so the next person has an equal challenge. Do this once your time is up. You will be given a paper and pad to take notes on what you find.

7) If at any point you are too frightened or there is a problem call me, I will be near the top of the stairs.

8) There are clues outside the house as well, explore the grounds. There are no clues in the house except for the basement. While someone is in the basement you should be outside.

9) If you find a red ticket, this is good for one reasonable yes/no question to me.

10) At the end of the evening, I will ask everyone to turn in a sheet a paper with their theory on what has happened. I will read these all aloud and the one with the closest story that has identified the murderer (if there was a murder) wins. The more detail, the better. Some samples:

Was there a murder, if so why, who, how?
Is Mr. Greinder dead or alive? Where is he or his body?
What was he doing?
Etc, etc, etc, etc...

For those that are first timers if there is a murderer, he or she is here. They know they are the murderer and will be trying to trick you!

This year the story was about a mad scientist. His obsession was to figure out a way to combine oil and water. His lab was in the basement of the house. He was a very introverted guy and did not want to be disturbed, so he would do things around the house to try to scare the kids away. Mr. Greinder actually did accomplish combining oil and water, but was murdered by his ex-partner who tried to steal his work.

What I did after creating the story line was to create a fake lab in the basement. This was quite involved, but it was fun. I sectioned off a portion of the basement, it was not a big section, about 20'x20'. I sectioned it off with a tarp and had streamers running from the stairs to this section of the basement. I took the light bulbs out so players could not turn on the lights and only could use the lantern. I also created a tape of spooky sounds using a sound effects CD. That took a while, but was worth it and I have used it a few times since. I used various types of sounds effects: foot steps, screams, etc and spaced them on the tape at random times. Some sounds were 30 seconds apart, 2 minutes, etc, you could never predict when a sound was coming. I hid this tape player behind the tarp and aimed it into the basement, not directly towards the 'lab' area, thus it was a little harder to tell from where the sounds were coming.

Four things made this year's mystery scary.
1) Darkness, always a scary issue.
2) Being alone in the dark makes it worse.
3) Spooky noises coming from someplace unknown in the dark.
4) The simple fear of not knowing what was going to happen.

Each player was handed the lantern as they started down the stairs to the basement, the door was shut behind them. I used an old locomotive signal lantern. It was basically a kerosene lamp. This was great to use since the natural flame was spookier. I gave them fifteen minutes and then called them back up. They had no idea what to expect when they went down. Was something or someone going to jump out at them? Was that the tape recorder or was someone else down there? Was that a shadow from the lantern or… ? You would think it would not be that scary, but people's imaginations will run away with them. I was surprised that just about every person who went down was at least spooked by something or other. One of the sounds gave them chills, or they just got nervous being alone, or they thought the lantern was going out, hmm? People really did get spooked, and it added a lot of atmosphere and fun to the game. But, back to the lab set up…

In the middle of the room was an old workbench that was in the basement, it was old and was perfect for the look I was going for. On that workbench, I put two old plastic microscopes I had since I was a kid, (pays to save everything sometimes). I put slides, jars and whatever I could scatter around to make it look like a lab. I also put one jar filled with water and the other with vegetable oil. I had a very old typewriter set up on a plastic milk crate in the corner, papers strewn everywhere. We had a bed down there that I pulled the mattress half off the box spring, so it would look even more disheveled. I was trying to give the impression of a struggle and that the basement/lab had not been used in a long time. I bought a bunch of fake spider/cob webs and draped them all over the place. I had a phone that was lying off the hook, strewn on the floor with fake blood on it. This phone was the murder weapon. When I was all finished, the scene looked really good.

One of the main clues that I used for the story line was a micro cassette recorder. I used a model that had variable speeds. It was used by Mr. Greinder to record his notes. The recorder was the type with a scrolling number counter. One of the clue sheets that I left lying in the lab had all the index numbers from the tape. If someone fast-forwarded the recorder to those portions of the tape, they could listen to a clue. These clues were recorded by me. I tried to disguise my voice and make it sound more like an old man. I muffled the microphone with cotton and talked slow, it seemed to work. The entries usually went something like this: "August 1st 1999, Today I made some advances in my studies, but I have been hounded by my ex-partner" Some were longer, but each entry had some small piece of the story line. There were two tapes, one I left in a corner, and the second was on a shelf. I left the tape recorder set to the fast speed, so the players first had to find the tapes and then figure out to use the recorder. Once a player did this, he/she now had to find and figure out the index system. Once they put in a tape and found an index spot with a recording on it, the tape would most likely be playing to fast to understand. Hitting the speed switch solved that problem.

To figure out who the murderer was, the players needed to figure our four clues, which would reveal the name of the murderer. Two of the clues were number puzzles (see below), the other clue was a key of the typewriter that was stuck pushed down, and finally there where three pieces of blood stained paper. If the pieces of paper where put together they would reveal a letter that was fingered in 'blood'.

As evidence that he was trying to scare the kids away, we had a hammock in the backyard. I tied a piece of fishing string to the end of the hammock and then ran it across the backyard and let it end near a basement window. If you pulled the string the hammock would rock back and forth. It was an easy clue to find, because someone would eventually get the fishing line wrapped around their feet when searching for clues in the yard.

On the following pages is one of the two puzzles I had the players solve. In the first picture you will see two pieces of Styrofoam. I drew the puzzle on the Styrofoam and then broke it in two.

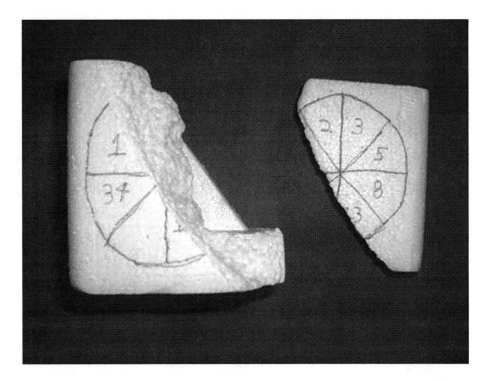

I hid the pieces and the players had to find the pieces and put them together. Obviously to make it harder I could have broken it into more pieces. Once the players put the two pieces together, they could now solve it.

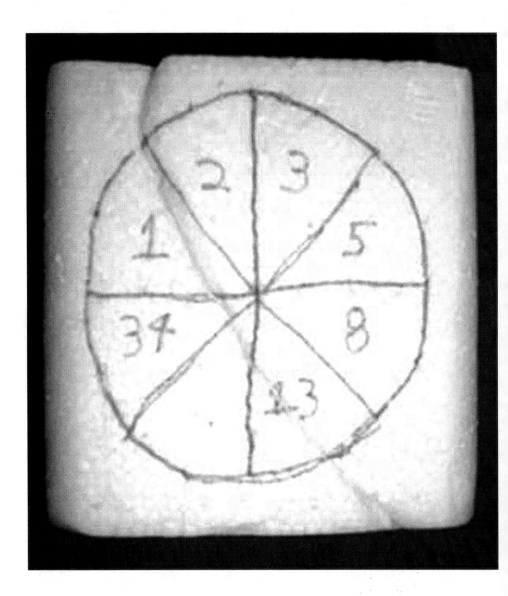

The solution to this puzzle gave them a number. This number could be found on a 'key' sheet that was also a clue. The number from the above puzzle was equated to a letter, giving them another hint at the killer's name. See end of book for answer.

The second puzzle was similar but this one was drawn on a piece of cardboard. As you can see in the picture below, I cut it up like a jigsaw puzzle.

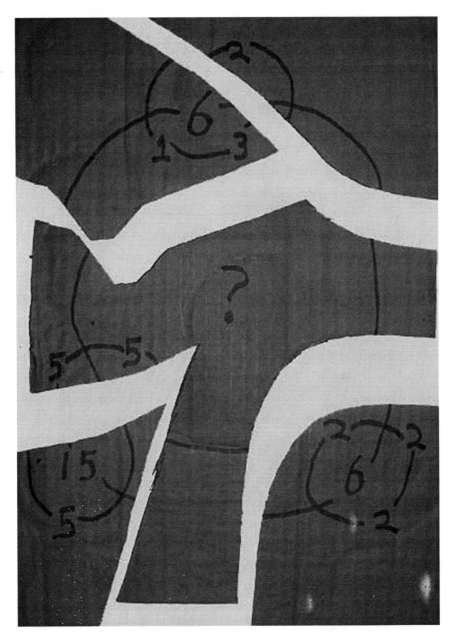

When the players found all five pieces they could assemble the cardboard puzzle. Once the pieces were all together it became another puzzle to solve. The question mark in the center is a number that can be solved from the other circles of numbers in the puzzle. The number that the players get from solving this puzzle can be used with a number key to find another letter of the killer's name. Assembled puzzle below and answer at the end of book.

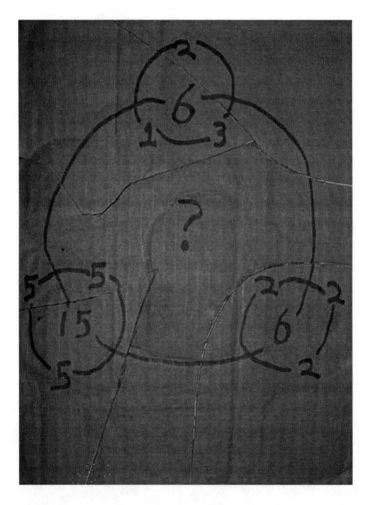

This year there was no 'body' so to say, but if players searched the garden they would find a glass jar. In the jar were ashes and a set of teeth. Players would have to assume the murderer burned up the body. For the teeth I just used a set of fake teeth you would use for a costume. It looked good once all the ashes got on them.

I always try to make the story line interesting and fit together. Even if some of the things are not directly related to solving the mystery, they still give it the feel of a real story. This also helps people in the end to piece together a good solution with detail. Mr. Griender had relationship problems related to his work. On a crumbled piece of paper in the corner of the room, the players would find this:

Dearest,

I know it has been many years since we have spoken, but I can't help still having feelings for you and wondering how things are going. I have met a very nice man and he treats me well, but he lacks your mind, the same thing that split us apart. You and that damned experiment. I told you it would drive you crazy and us apart. It's nature, you can not change nature. If you need or want to talk to me the door is still open for a little while longer.
Your love...

It gives Mr. Griender some more personality and gives a tiny clue to help them figure out what he was trying to do (Water and oil, remember?).

I also had papers scattered around the floor. As the story developed, Mr. Griender's ex-partner was trying to steal his final report on his success of getting oil and water to mix. So, I pulled out my chemistry books and on various pieces of paper wrote down some things that would sound very scientific, such as:

As you can see from the above calculations, the process was fairly simple once I broke through the covalent bonds. To conclude, I

I had a number of these incomplete pages scattered around the typewriter, giving the impression of scraps that were cast aside. This really sets up the mood and sparks people's interest. I also had a number of science books scattered about, some with bookmarks in them at pages related to water and/or oil. I even had a child psychology book to help them figure out that he was trying to scare the kids away.

In total there were four clues/puzzles the players need to solve to get the murderer's name. The murderer's name was only four letters and the clues again were as follows:

1) Typewriter key stuck in a down position gave a letter.
2) Blood stained paper gave a letter.

3) Styrofoam puzzle gave a number that coincided with a letter on a number letter key.
4) Cardboard puzzle gave a number that coincided with a letter on a number letter key.

Also, always have a fire extinguisher around if you are going to use a live flame lantern. Someone could have tripped or accidentally set something off, especially because the basement was so dark.

The problem with this party was that some people were getting really anxious to get back downstairs to find more clues and explore. If I ever did this type of murder mystery again, I would also have clues in other parts of the house. But some people still consider this the best murder mystery to date. This also brings up another point. Different people will like different types of games. Some people will like hard clues, some will like a good story line, some will like acting, etc. Try not to focus on that too much, change them up year after year and you all will have a good time. If you hit on a combination that everyone likes, take a closer look at it and try to figure out the right combination for your particular group of friends.

MYSTERY AT LAKE JONEST
Sample Game Four

The fourth sample game that I included in this book was the most difficult to play and create at the time of writing this book. I did a little research about the area where I lived to see what would come up and spark some ideas. I found out about Indian tribes that used to live in the area and also found out about the man after whom the area was named. It also said he was forced to leave his land behind during the Civil War. I liked both of these interesting facts of history and wondered if I could combine them in any way? Indians brought to mind Indian curses. And someone who had to leave his land behind might have left something valuable. In the end I came up with the following 'history' of the area. Keep in mind that about ninety percent of this is true.

A Brief History of Lake Jonest

The original residents of Lake Jonest were the Doe and Necostin Indians of the Algonquin tribes (Anacostia derives its name from the Necostins). Artifacts of these early natives are still occasionally found. The Jonest Community was named in memory of a wealthy doctor who built his home here and also operated a mill. The man was Dr. John W. Jonest, originally from New Jersey. In 1849 Dr. Jonest came to our area and built both a home and a mill on Columbia Pike at Holmes Run very near the present dam. He practiced medicine throughout the surrounding community and ran his mill up to the time of the Civil War.

During its retreat from the Battle of Bull Run, the Union Army overran Dr. Jonest's home. His property was so damaged that he was forced to flee north and planned to return at the end of the war. He never lived long enough to do so.

The Lake Jonest we know came into being in 1915. An increasing need for water by the City of Alexandria led the Alexandria Water Company to build the dam and establish a reservoir to store the waters from the branches of Holmes Run. Dam construction was begun in 1913 under contract with the Piedmont Construction Company. Specifications for the Jonest Dam were complex and the construction was massive. A railway was built to transport the masonry stones to the dam site. The contractor went broke completing the job.

The result was a dam 400 feet wide with the spillway at the top 205 feet above mean sea level and 68 feet above the streambed. Behind this dam there formed a lake of 135 acres and over five miles of shoreline. In the time that followed the 750 acres of shoreline were divided into 1,020 lots on which now stand 1,000 homes.

In the early 1920s there was reportedly a rumor spreading around the lake that during the dam construction a few gold coins were found. It was this reason the dam construction took longer than it should have, as the contractor spent time seeking the source of the gold coins. Others say that an old Indian curse was causing problems during the dam construction and still others say both reasons caused the delays.

Game Play and Rules

Welcome to the fourth annual murder mystery. Here is some basic game information.

Your job is to find out who the murderer is, why he or she did it, and any other details surrounding the murder and the reason for it. The more details you can figure out the better. At the end of the evening everyone will be given a piece of paper and will write down who they think the murderer is and why. To avoid a tie (usually more than one person knows who did it), write down as many additional things you believe were involved in the murder.

In case you are wondering, the murderer is someone at the party. He or she knows they are the murderer and their job is to attempt to confuse, lie and thwart your effort to solve the mystery without being detected. If no one can ID the murderer at the end of the night, he or she wins the game. Trust no one!

In the course of the evening you will be finding red tickets scattered about. These entitle you to ask me one yes or no question at my discretion. Find as many of these as possible and ask me questions at any time.

The game takes place at our house, there are references to other places around Lake Jonest, but there is no need to go to these places.

The game clues and other items can be found either outside, in the den (ground floor) and in the living room/dinning room areas. There is nothing in the two upper levels of the house (bedrooms, upstairs bathrooms) or basement that has anything to do with the mystery.

The red shed in the yard near the pond has nothing in it related to the mystery, don't waste time trying to get in there.

The pond- please do not jump/dive in the pond, throw anything in the pond, drink the water, pore additional liquids in it, spit in it, yell at it, detonate explosives in it or urinate in it. Fish are currently living in there. If you think something must be done with the pond, please ask me first. The large rocks immediately surrounding the pond do not contain/hide any clues.

As far as any other actions that may be considered damaging or defacing to the house and or surrounding area, such as digging or breaking something, please ask me first. If something like this needs to be done, I can tell you if you are on the right track before it's too late. Anyone found cheating or trying to 'get around' solving a puzzle will be burned at the stake and then removed from game play.

Most of all, have fun, enjoy...

I will concentrate mainly on the ideas I came up with and used this year. The story was long and complex, as well as solving the mystery. Hopefully these ideas will help you generate more of your own.

The basic story as stated above, was that the Indians put a curse on the land and gold that was hidden there. I switched it up and used Mayan culture instead of Indian during the story. A stretch, of course, but I found more interesting ideas about the Mayans when I searched the Internet.

The only way to get the gold to reveal itself was through a sacrifice and finding its exact location. The sacrifice had already been taken care of, and this was the murder. There was no body this year, only a newspaper report that I created and the players could find indicating that a headless body was found in the lake near the house. The murderer just did not have time to finish deciphering the clues to find the exact location of the treasure.

For some maps, I used the architectural lot plan of our property to indicate various markings around the house and yard. I used various pieces of information about Mayan and Indian culture. Below are some examples of information I was able to find on the Internet. I used these as clues and as parts of the story line in the murder mystery.

Below is an example of hieroglyphics. For the clues, I had items circled in the pictures. Players would later be able to find deciphering sheets to try to figure out what the pictures meant.

Below are some perfect examples of how you can use symbols to create clues. By using the symbols below, you can create some primitive sentences. These are just a few I found on line at 'Rabbit In The Moon', www.halfmoon.org. Also included are symbols representing numbers.

BIRTH

u kab panamil
s/he touched
the earth

huliy
s/he arrived
(also used in
other ways)

RANK

hok'
to take
office

chumwan
he was
seated

ahaw ??
became ahaw

pat sak hun tu ba
he tied the white
headband on himself
(crowned himself)

WAR

"star over"
war event verb

 blank can contain
"yi", "kah" (place),
or the name of the
location of the battle

chak
to destroy,
decapitate

puluy
was
burned

hubi
to bring down
(also used in
other ways)

 chucheh
he was
captured

 ???
to be
wounded

DEATH

ochiy bih
to enter
the road

ochiy bih
to enter
the road

kimi
s/he died

 k'ayi u sak niknal
his/her white
flower ended

 hil
to expire

 u bah ti way
s/he went
sleeping

 mukah
s/he was
buried

CEREMONIES

u chok ch'ah
he scatters
sacred drops

ch'am
to harvest,
let blood

tzak
to conjure
(a spirit)

tzutz or hom
it was completed
(period ending)

 nawah
to be
adorned

 ch'am
to grasp
(object)

och k'ak'
smoke entered
(building dedication)

OTHER

u bah
s/he goes,
does,
performs

 ak'ot
to dance

tz'ap
to erect,
set up

yilah
s/he saw,
visited

pat
to make

tz'ap
to set

kuch
to carry

 tal
to come

66

COLORS AND DIRECTIONS

k'an
(yellow)

yax
(green, blue)

sak
(white)

ek'
(black)

chak
(red)

xaman
(north)

lak'in
(east)

nohol?
(south)

chik'in
(west)

northeast

southeast

northwest

southwest

(drawn by David Stuart)

NON-FAMILY RELATIONSHIPS

u chan
(his captive
or ward)

u bak
(his captive
or bone)

u sahal
(his
subordinate)

y-ahawte
(his vassal
lord)

u kahi
(under his
auspices)

u way
(his companion
spirit)

y-ichnal
(together
with)

y-etel
(and,
together with)

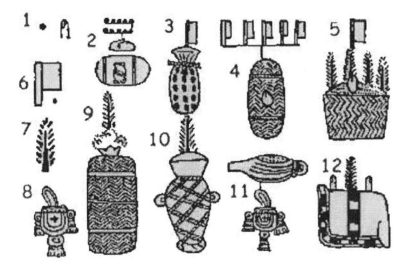

I also found a number of words representing phrases and numbers, once again, perfect for clues and decode sheets.

1 - ce
2 - ome
3 - yei
4 - nahui
5 - macuilli
6 - chicuace
7 - chicome
8 - chicueyi
9 - chicnahui
10 - matlactli
11 - matlactli huan ce
12 - matlactli huan ome
13 - matlactli huan yei
14 - matlactli huan nahui
15 - caxtolli
16 - caxtolli huan ce
17 - caxtolli huan ome
18 - caxtolli huan yei
19 - caxtolli huan nahui
20 - cempualli
21 - cempualli huan ce
22 - cempualli huan ome
23 - cempualli huan yei
24 - cempualli huan nahui
25 - cempualli huan macuilli
26 - cempualli huan chicuace
27 - cempualli huan chicome
28 - cempualli huan chicueyi
29 - cempualli huan chicnahui
30 - cempualli huan matlactli
31 - cempualli huan matlactli huan ce
32 - cempualli huan matlactli huan ome
33 - cempualli huan matlactli huan yei
34 - cempualli huan matlactli huan nahui
35 - cempualli huan matlactli huan macuilli
36 - cempualli huan matlactli huan chicuace
37 - cempualli huan matlactli huan chicome

The Panther Passing Across--Tecumseh
He Makes a Loud Noise--Lalawethika
A Door Opened--Sauwaseekau Kumskaka
Gives Light as He Walks--Wapameepto Methoataske
Changing Feathers--Penagashea
Stand Firm--Wasabogoa
Flying Clouds--Payakootha
Black Fish--Chiungalla
Blue Jacket--Wehyahpiherhnwah
Big Turtle--Sheltowee
Black Beard--Wesecahnay
Blanket Man--Aquewelene Apetotha
Yellow Hawk--Outhowwa Shokka
Bad Spirit--Matchemenetoo
Little Moon--Matchsquathi Tebethto
Tame Hawk--Kekewapilethy Ptweowa
Wild Cat--Peshewa
Fireheart—Skootekitehi

Shooting Star—Tecuma
The Open Door—Tenskwatawa
A Cat that Flies in the Air—

Turtle Laying Its Eggs—

White Hawk—Waupee
Red Pole—Misquacoonaw
Cornstalk—Hokolesqua
Black Hoof—Catahecassa
Long Shanks—Waytheah
Big Horn--Spemica Lawba
Black Snake—Shementeo
Child in a Blanket--Aquewa

Duck Eggs—Sheshepukwawala
Little Sun--Matchsquathi Kisathoi
Black Stump—Chiuxca
Great White Wolf--Psaiwiwuhkernekah

Cold Water--Wepe-nipe

Family Relationships

My father--no'tha
Your father--ko'tha
My mother—neegah
Mother--nik-yah
My brother--ni-je-ni-nuh
(blood)Brother--jai-nai-nah
My son--ni-kwith-ehi
My sister--ni-t-kweem-a
My daughter--ni-da-ne-thuh
Daughter--Dah-nai-tha
My husband--ni-da-ne-thuh

Numbers

One--Negate
Two--Neshwa
Three--Nithese
Four--Newe
Five--Nialinwe
Six--Negotewathe

The following sheet is a good example of how I used these in one case during this murder mystery. This was found at the 'Native American Indian Resources' at http://www.kstrom.net/isk/mainmenu.html#mainmenutop.

70

	Important	Discovery!	
0			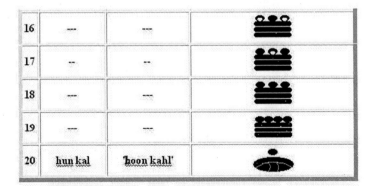
1	hun	'hoon'	
2	ka	'kah'	
3	ox	'ohsh'	
4	kan	'kahn'	
5	ho	'ho'	
6	uac	'wahk'	
7	uuc	'wook'	
8	uaxac	'washahk'	
9	bolon	'bohlohn'	
10	la hun	'lah hoon'	
11	buluk	'boolook'	
12	la ka	'lah kah'	
13	ox la hun	'ohsh lah hoon'	
14	--	--	
15	---	---	
16	---	---	
17	--	--	
18	---	---	
19	---	---	
20	hun kal	'hoon kahl'	

This sheet was cut in two (hence the cut between 15 and 16) and hidden as a clue. Also hidden as the party progressed were pieces of the three-piece puzzle I created from some pieces of plywood and an engraver. See below.

When the players combined the above completed puzzle with the key above, they got a string of numbers. 6,18,1,14,3,9 and 19. If these are matched up with letters of the alphabet, for example, 1 = A, then the last name of the murderer is spelled out. F-R-A-N-C-I-S in this case.

This was a stretch and only one player thought of matching the numbers to the alphabet.

The most complex thing about this murder mystery was the molds I created out of plaster. The first mold I created was from a skull drinking cup I found during Halloween. I cut the cup about a quarter of the way down. I blew up a small balloon and held it in the middle of the bottom portion of the mold and pored the plaster around it, filling it to the top. The balloon created a space in the skull. I filled the top portion of the mold to make the top of the skull. I took a key (I will explain what that key is for in a minute) and sealed in the skull. This skull is the skull represented in the picture on picture clue on page 15. See pictures on the following page for actual skull. Notice the crack along the top, this was sealed up with more plaster after the key was placed inside.

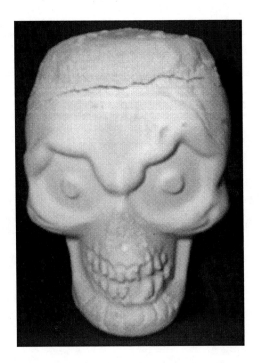

The next picture is of the open mold after I started gluing it back together for this book. Using the C-clamp on it broke it into a few pieces.

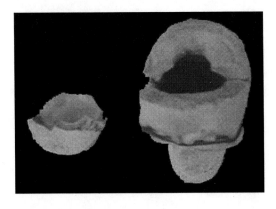

The next mold I made was also of a skull, but only of the face. This mold I came about by chance and was included as a protective cover for a singing skeleton Halloween decoration. In an old box of electrical parts, I had an electrical switch that was turned on and off with a key.

This is the key that was hidden in the plaster skull. I molded the skull around the key switch and attached electrical cords to it. See picture below.

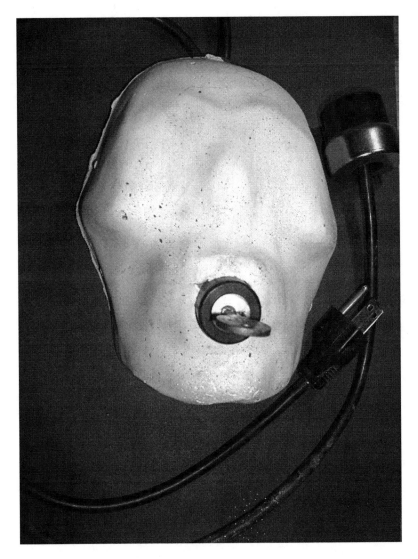

The players were trying to find a murderer and discover why a sacrifice was needed, but also locate the treasure. We have a fishpond in my yard. The fishpond has an electrical pump that drives a filter and waterfall. I had a bag full of pennies, which was tied to a long string and attached to a small balloon. I lodged this balloon in the output hose of the pump, under the water. The chain of events that occur to enable the players to find the treasure was:

1) Figure out there was treasure.
2) Find all pieces of the paper on paper clue and assemble to see diagram of skull and key
   inside.
3) Find C-clamp
4) Figure out to use C-clamp to break open skull and retrieve key.
5) Using maps and clues, figure out where skull with key switch is buried.
6) Uncover skull and use key.
7) Notice that once key is turned, pond begins running and a balloon has surfaced.
8) Retrieve balloon and see attached string, keep pulling string until treasure is pulled
   from pond.

As you can see this year was a complicated murder mystery to create and definitely to play. It is still remembered as the most difficult. While I was pleased with the props I created and the story line, in hindsight, I should have placed more clues directly related to solving the mystery. I had put out lots of 'filler' information and in the end it was hard for the players to determine which clues where most important. The following party is much easier to create and play.

MARIE LAVEAU
Sample Game Five

This sample game turned out to be one of the most fun games to play, for both the players and I. What was a little different about this game is that the players got to do a little acting and had to interact with each other in various instances. Lets begin with the rule sheet I handed out to the players.

Game Play and Rules

Welcome to the fifth annual murder mystery. Here are some basic game and rule information for this year's game.

Your job is simple, find out what is going on.

One very important thing to know is that the murderer is at the party and they know they are the murderer. Their job is to attempt to confuse, lie and thwart your effort to solve the mystery without being detected. They will be trying to stop you from catching them by what ever means the game allows.

It is your choice if you want to work alone or on a team. But one piece of advice is to mingle, you might need to know things about each other to find the murderer.

Things that you might ask yourself are:

Was there a murder?
Who was it?
Why?
Where is the body?
Murder weapon?
Motive?
Etc...

The more details you can figure out about the entire mystery
the better.
At the end of the evening everyone will be given a piece of paper and will write down who they think the murderer is and why. To avoid a tie (usually more than one person knows who did it), write down as many additional things you believe were involved in the murder and why it was done.

If no one can ID the murderer at the end of the night, the murderer will win the game.

In the course of the evening you will be finding red tickets scattered about. These entitle you to ask me one yes or no question at my discretion. Find as many of these as possible and ask me questions at any time.

The game clues and other items can be found either outside, in the den (ground floor) and in the living room/dinning room areas. There is nothing in the two upper levels of the house (bedrooms, upstairs bathrooms) or basement that has anything to do with the mystery.

The red shed in the yard near the pond has nothing in it this year related to the mystery; don't waste time trying to get in there.

The pond, please do not jump/dive in the pond, throw anything in the pond, drink the water, pore additional liquids in it, spit in it, yell at it, detonate explosives in it or urinate in it. Fish are currently living in there.

If you think something must be done with the pond, dug up, destroyed, chopped down, etc please ask me first, since past mysteries have included some of these possibilities. If something like this needs to be done I can tell you if you are on the right track before its too late.

The large rocks immediately surrounding the pond do not contain/hide any clues.

The big difference this year is that almost everyone will have to do a little acting.
During the game, things may happen to you. Once you have been informed please come see me for advice on what to do. Do not tell others, since part of the fun will be for them to figure out what has happened to you and what to do. Also, you CAN NOT FIX YOURSELF (you will understand later). So kick your creativity and imagination into high gear and have some fun when and if you need to.

Because of this addition to game play, an acting award will be presented at the end of the evening.

Anyone found cheating or trying to 'get around' solving a puzzle will be burned at the stake and then removed from game play.
Most of all have fun, enjoy and as usual...

Trust no one!

As you can see, this game is going to run a little differently than the previous ones. The main difference is, during this game the players can have curses placed on them. I will cover this in more detail later on. I also gave the players one clue to begin:

Marie Laveau

Believed to be born in New Orleans in 1794 and
died in New Orleans on June 15th, 1881. A free
women of color as well as a Quadroon (African,
Indian, French, Spanish), she became the most
famous and powerful Voodoo Queen in the world,
so powerful the she proclaimed herself the pope
of Voodoo in the 1830s. She was respected and
feared by thousands including the Catholic
Church. A devout catholic, going to mass each
day, she got permission to hold rituals behind
St. Louis Cathedral. Starting out as a
hairdresser and later as a selfless nurse,
Marie Laveau became the first commercial Voodoo
Queen. She had fifteen children by her second
husband, one of which (Marie Philomene Laveau
Glapion) walked in her footsteps and became
almost as powerful as her mother.

Voodoo is the main theme of this game. I did a number of things differently this time. As mentioned, I gave people the chance to act by means of being cursed. I also did not have a body, so to say, this year. Basically one of the players, the murderer, is a descendant of Marie Laveau. She was able to raid the tomb of Marie and steal a spell to shrink money. She is the only person that can shrink it and then enlarge it again, rendering any shrunken money useless. I bought a pack of miniature money bills and used those as my props. For the spell to work, she must capture the soul of a human and use it, rendering them undead. I picked another player to be the zombie/victim. This gave them an opportunity to act as well, since as the night wore on, the player began to 'decay' and act more zombie like. When I met with the players, I explained to him what he was to do and that I hid some zombie makeup in the bathroom. About every half hour I asked him to go apply some more makeup and become more zombie like. This added entertainment and bewildered players.

Back to the curses, I laid these out along with clues. I made them look the same, so you never knew if you were getting a clue or a curse. The idea was that the murderer was laying the curses around to scare people away, so that the players would not find out her secret. Of course I also had 'cures' for the curses. For all the sheets, I burned the edges and put voodoo doll graphics on them for effect.

From Fast To Slow
You Will Now Go
For You Time Now Passes
As Slow As Molasses

You have been cursed with the
"Curse Of Molasses"

As mentioned in the introduction that I handed out to the players, when they got cursed and were not sure what to do, I just told them to come ask me. With this one, they had to move in slow motion. I would let it go on for about 15 minutes before I would hide the cure someplace. The cure is as follows.

Cure For Molasses:

Have a Seat On the Eternal
Fire Of Speed For Two Minutes

Witnesses Must Be Present

The last part is important, since the whole fun of it would be lost. The 'Eternal Fire Of Speed' was also on a separate piece of paper that was hidden, so the cure was really two fold. Remember, there is the curse, the cure and the prop. There are three 'parts' to these curses. Once they found both and made the match, the player could be cured by following the directions. Things got really funny as multiple people were cursed at the same time all trying to cure each other. A rule I also put into place, was that players could not cure themselves.

Eternal Fire Of Speed

81

There were a number of curses, so let me start by getting those out of the way. The following is a list of all the curses that were 'cast' that evening, their cures and any item that was additionally needed.

Darkness Sets In
Living A Nightmare
The Sight You See
You Can Not Bare

You have been cursed with the
"Curse Of Fear"

Cure For Fear:

Go To Pond, Keep Back Towards House,
Sit On Ground, Close Your Eyes and
Cover Face With Hands. Count Slowly to
Twenty-Five. Don't Move, Stop Counting Or Look,
NO MATTER WHAT YOU FEEL OR HEAR!!!

We have a fishpond in the back of our yard, it is the furthest and darkest portion of our yard from the house. The main idea here is just to get them nervous. This obviously will vary depending on your house layout, but once they hide their eyes, start rustling about so they wonder what is going to happen.

Nothing You Can Do
There Is No Hope
Don't Even Try
You Can't Cope

You have been cursed with the
"Curse Of Low Self Esteem"

Cure For Low Self Esteem:

Take The World Between
Thy Hands And Squeeze
While Saying Allowed
"I Think I Can,
I Think I Can"

Three Times...

Witnesses Must Be Present

For this cure, I hide a small rubber ball that looked like the earth, once someone made the connection and the above was followed, the curse was lifted.

Scratchy Throat
Never Ending
Cough And Cough
There Is No Defending

You have been cursed with the
"Curse Of Coughing"

Cure For Coughing:

Loll Of Soothing

Witnesses Must Be Present

I hide an envelope marked "Loll Of Soothing" and placed a lollypop in it. Once they started sucking on it, the curse was lifted.

Why Are You Here
What Is Your Name
Suddenly You Don't
Feel The Same

You have been cursed with the
"Curse Of Amnesia"

Cure For Amnesia:

Hold A Brain Against Your
Head and Repeat,
"I Remember It All"
Three Times...

Witnesses Must Be Present

For this curse, the additional prop was a small rubber brain I picked up in a 25-cent machine.

Rotten Eggs
Tougher And Tougher
Holding Your Nose
Will Still Cause You
To Suffer

You have been cursed with the
"Curse Of Stink"

Cure For Stink:

Rub The Hair Of A Black Limbed Voodoo Doll Under Your Nose

Witnesses Must Be Present

This prop was another toy from a 25-cent machine. It was a small plastic doll with long hair. I colored the arms of the doll with a marker.

Eyes Heavy As Lead Body Feeling Weak The Time Has Come For You To Sleep

You have been cursed with the "Curse Of Sleep"

Cure For Sleep:

The Ringing Of The Giant Golden Bell While Two Witnesses Whisper "Wake Up" In Your Ears

Witnesses Must Be Present

For this prop, I used a very large boat bell I had. It made a very load ring when shaken.

Tongue Tied and Tongue Twisted
Your Ability To Speak Has Now
Been Lifted

You have been cursed with the
"Curse Of Silence"

Cure For Silence:

Three Tablets Of Speech

Witnesses Must Be Present

In an envelope labeled "Tablets of Speech" I had three pieces of candy.

From The Depths Of Darkness
From The Depths Of Your Soul
Your Saddest Of Times
Now Unfolds

You have been cursed with the
"Curse Of Sadness"

Cure For Sadness:

What can run but never walks,
has a mouth but never talks,
has a bed but never sleeps,
has a head but never weeps?

The Answer Must Be Said Allowed
Three Times...

Witnesses Must Be Present

The answer to this riddle is a river.

Pressure From All Sides
No Room To Move
Locked In A cage
You're Filled With Rage

You have been cursed with the
"Curse Of Rage"

Cure For Rage:

The Only Cure For Rage Is
To Have Ice Pressed Against
The Back Of The Suffers Neck
By Surprise. The Person Applying
The Ice Must Sing Part Of The
Lyrics To 'Cool', From
West Side Story, Allowed.
"Boy, Boy, Crazy Boy. Get Cool Boy
Keep Coolly Cool Boy!"

Witnesses Must Be Present

Piercing To The Top
From Deep Inside
Like A Burning Flame
Suffer, The Curse Of Pain

You have been cursed with the
"Curse Of Pain"

Cure For Pain:

A Band-Aid Marked with
Silver Must Be Stuck Upon
The Forehead

Witnesses Must Be Present
Once again, I labeled an envelope and placed a band-aid in it.

No Matter What Is True
Don't Even Try
You Are Now Only Capable
Of Telling A Lie

You have been cursed with the
"Curse Of Lying"

Cure For Lying:

Burn A Pair Of Pants

Witnesses Must Be Present

Liar liar pants on fire. Use a cut out from a magazine or clip art like the one below. Put this prop out early; it will help to avoid coming outside to a burning pair of someone's real pants.

As Stiff As A Board
No longer Free
Your Leg Is Now
Locked At The Knee

You have been cursed with the
"Curse Of Stiff Leg"

Cure For Stiff Leg:

The Paw Of An Alligator
Placed Upon The Knee

Witnesses Must Be Present

For this cure I had an alligator claw key chain.

—

Pepper In Your Nose
Bugs Under Your Skin
The Need To Scratch
Will Now Begin

You have been cursed with the
"Curse Of Itch"

Cure For Itch:

How Does A Dog Get Rid Of Fleas?

Repeat Answer Three Times...

Witnesses Must Be Present

Answer: They Start from scratch!

Power Of Dead Sight:

Rise From The Ground
Secret Spirits

Have Now Been Found
With That Said
You Can Now See the Dead

This is actually a very good and powerful 'curse'. This will enable the player to see the zombie as what he or she really is. Once someone got this curse, I told them that Mark (The player that was the zombie (walking dead) was glowing. From that point on they should figure it out from what the curse enables them to do.

Power To Place A Curse:

To Help With Your Chores
Powers Of Voodoo
Are Now Yours

With This Power You Can
Curse Anyone Playing The
Game For Ten Minutes

Witnesses Must Be Present

This is also a very good one to find. The one I usually would suggest to the player is the curse of truth. They can ask a player any question they want other than the big one, "Are you the Murder?" The most popular was, "Are you hiding any clues?"

Power To Place A Good Spell:

To Help With A Good Deed
Powers Of Voodoo
Are All You Need

With This Power You Can
Place A Good Spell On Anyone Playing The
Game For Ten Minutes

Witnesses Must Be Present

This one was typically used out of sympathy for a player whom was not cured of their cures for an extended amount of time.

As a little extra, I had an empty jar floating in the fishpond. In there was the zombies soul. If someone found the clue stating that was were the soul was, and let the zombie breath back in his soul, he was brought back from the dead. If someone opened the jar before they knew what was in there, the soul was lost forever as was the case with this party. The players, while getting cursed and cured, had to figure out that the murderer was a direct descendant of Marie. I gave them lots of hints such as copies of emails the murderer wrote, letters from the Louisiana Genealogical & History Society, copies of web searches, etc, etc. If they put all this together they would figure out, which at this party most people did, that the murderer was a direct descendant of Marie.
For the player to understand the motive and why they were finding miniature pieces of money around, I had a number of these clues also floating around:

There has been a modern day folk tale that
Marie Laveau created a powerful spell to
protect her money. The spell simply shrunk the
money to a smaller size, making it useless for
anyone but her. When she needed to use the
money she simply reversed the spell.
The tale goes on to say that Marie took this
spell to her grave, literally. One night a few
years ago her tomb was broken into, yet no one
knows what exactly was stolen.
Some say it was the money spell, others say it
was just souvenir hunters. Why does anyone
care? Simple, the main ingredient for the spell
to work is a human soul.

This should have started players on making connections about what was going on.

For the players to figure out who the murderer was, I had three puzzles and one indirect clue for them to figure out.

The first puzzle was the letter "B" written on a sheet of paper. I cut this paper into about six pieces and hid them around. Once all the pieces were found, it could be put back together to reveal the letter.

The second puzzle was a Stereogram. A stereogram is one of those pictures that you stare at and another picture will appear when your eyes try to focus. I found a web site that allowed you to create your own stereograms and print them out. So I created one for the letter "E".

The third was a simple key, once again using the alphabet. On the key was printed A=1, B=2, C-3, etc. On another sheet of paper was printed "J-I=__" The answer is 1 which equals A.

The final clue was a page out of a dictionary. The page was just for the letter "N".

If the players put all this together as well as what all the players last names were, they would come up with the last name of "BEAN". That was the murderer.

That completes the last of the Sample games. I wish you luck in creating your own murder mystery games. Just remember to be creative, challenging and most of all, have fun!

Answers to puzzles on pages 44 and 45 are 21 and 27 respectively.

362524